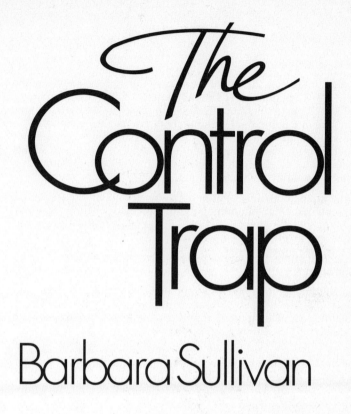

# The Control Trap

## Barbara Sullivan

BETHANY HOUSE PUBLISHERS
MINNEAPOLIS, MINNESOTA 55438

*The Control Trap*
Copyright © 1991
Barbara Sullivan

Published by Bethany House Publishers
A Ministry of Bethany Fellowship International
11400 Hampshire Avenue South
Minneapolis, Minnesota 55438
www.bethanyhouse.com

Printed in the United States of America by
Bethany Press International, Minneapolis, Minnesota 55438

**Library of Congress Cataloging-in-Publication Data**

Sullivan, Barbara A.
    The control trap / Barbara Sullivan.
       p.   cm.
    Includes bibliographical references.

     1. Control (Psychology)—Religious aspects—Christianity.
2. Women—Religious life.  I. Title.
BV4527.S83   1991
248.8'43—dc20                           90–24040
ISBN 1–55661–169–2                      CIP

To my husband, John,
who put up with this "controlling woman"
and lovingly demonstrated a better way—
trusting in a sovereign God.

BARBARA SULLIVAN and her husband, John, are parents of four grown children and reside in South Holland, Illinois. Together they pioneered an interdenominational fellowship that now includes a Christian grammar school and a "seminary for street people"—a Christian discipling center for recovered inner-city drug addicts. For ten years, Barbara has led a ministry team into a state drug treatment center for Bible study and evangelism.

In addition to her work in the fellowship and multiple speaking engagements, she is a certified aerobics instructor who leads classes for the church and a local health club. She is a graduate of Loyola University of Chicago and has authored four books, including *First Born, Second Born*.

# *Contents*

## Section 1
### Discovering Control

## Section 2
### Becoming "The Director"

## Section 3
### Why Do We Control?

## Section 4
### Family Ties That Bind

## Section 5
### Spiritual Roots and Release

✱*mothering a husband 48*

# Section 1

# DISCOVERING CONTROL

*We can make our plans, but the final outcome is in God's hands.*

Proverbs 16:1, TLB

# 1

# *The Letter*

I was clearing the breakfast dishes when I heard the *plunk* of letters dropping in the mailbox. As I rifled through the stack of mail, I noticed the return address on one envelope addressed to me. It was from John, the oldest of our four children, who lives just twenty minutes away in downtown Chicago. *Strange*, I thought, *John has never written me before. He always calls to check in. I hope nothing's wrong.*

Tearing open the letter I read:

Dear Mom,

It's three A.M., and I've just finished reading R. C. Sproul's book *Johnny, Come Home.* . . .

I smiled. I'd bought the book for John three years before, hoping it would have a spiritual impact on him. It had remained on his shelf, gathering dust—until now.

John went on to write how the book had touched him: "It opened my eyes to my spiritual state." He ended with the words that are a healing balm to every mother who has ever prayed for a wandering child: "I cried, because I'm so far from 'home.' Please pray for me."

I cried intermittently the rest of the day—*cried*, because I saw God's faithfulness to me and remembered the many times I had doubted Him. Even worse, at times I'd accused Him of not caring about me or my son.

Several years before, John had shown signs that his once-vibrant faith was growing cold. Church had become a bore. My husband John, who is a pastor, had to be careful not to give spiritual advice. Spiritual growth was not on our son's agenda. I began a campaign to bring John back to God.

Not only did I panic, I bombarded heaven with my prayers and demands. Just in case God ran out of ideas, I told Him ways he could reach John. When I saw Sproul's book *Johnny, Come Home* in a Christian bookstore one day, I *knew* it was meant for my John. On his next drop-in at home, I presented it to him. Then I waited for the reaction.

Nothing.

I grew angry. I'd done my part; why wasn't God doing His?

The book sat ignored on the shelf until John's God, not his mother, knew the time was right to open his heart. My motive was right; my timing—and maybe even my method—was all wrong. Sadly, the book was only one of my clever needlings at John about his faith.

The letter before me was filled with God's reminder between each line, *Why don't you trust John to me?*

I cried tears of gratitude to God for His faithfulness, and tears of remorse for my rather shabby manipulations. I was delighted with what God had done, and also humbled. If John had read the book when I first gave it to him, it probably would have been just another nice inspirational book from his "concerned," insistent mother. God knew the exact time that John would "connect" with the book. He won out in spite of my desperate attempts to coerce John back to faith.

I found it so easy to rationalize my desire to control the people in my life. My son, for example—surely it was right and good that he renew his spiritual commitment, wasn't it? And surely an occasional "nudge in the right direction" wasn't bad, was it? John's letter got my attention in an unexpected way, and I began to rethink my assumptions about those questions. At the time I could not deal with the possibility that I was also trying to protect the family reputation—the pastor's son "out of the fold." What would people think?

I know that I am not alone in my desire to control. My husband and I have pastored a church that began in our home nearly twenty years ago. We have grown into a suburban church of some 300 adults, with a satellite church in inner-city Chicago, a rehabilitation center for ex-drug addicts, and a Christian grammar school. So in my position as the pastor's wife, I counsel wives, mothers, and grandmothers from *very* different backgrounds. In spite of the diversity, they are one in the emotional, relational, and spiritual problems they suffer.

"How do I give up trying to arrange everything in my family's life or circumstances and trust God?" This kind of question arises in probably seventy-five percent of my counseling sessions with women.

## An Answer That Was No Answer

Certainly the issue of control is not exclusively a "woman's problem." You no doubt are aware, as I am, of families where a husband or father is out of balance and overbearing with his wife and children. But the problem of control has intensified among women, I believe, because of the fallout from the feminist movement that began in 1963 with Betty Friedan's book *The Feminine Mystique*. Friedan insisted that "something is very wrong with the way American women are trying to live their lives today."[1]

To Friedan, what was wrong with us was our *men*: We women needed to *seize control*. Ironically, three decades later, there is still "something wrong."

Dr. Susan Jeffers, a former feminist, writes that women today are "being run by the same insecurities, fears, and expectations that ran women's lives years ago."[2] She concludes that "while healthy relationships were difficult prior to the women's movement, for too many of us, they seem to be impossible today."[3]

To me, this indicates an attitude permeating our culture, and I believe we Christian women must be aware of it. In attempting to take control of their lives, many women have adopted the attitude that their true enemy is *men*. Dr. Jeffers runs workshops on relationships and does one exercise that brings telling results. She seats men on one side of the room and women on the other. Then she encourages them to ask questions. "Generally speaking the men seem to have an at-

---

[1]Betty Friedan, *The Feminine Mystique* (New York: Dell Publishing, 1963), p. 7.
[2]Susan Jeffers, *Opening Our Hearts to Men* (New York: Ballantine Books, 1989), p. 15.
[3]Ibid., pp. 19–20.

titude of sincere inquiry: 'What do women look for in a man?' 'How do women feel about splitting the check?' . . . and so on. What comes through is a desire to please women, combined with a total confusion as to what women really want."[4]

The women, however, ask very different questions. "They sit forward in their chairs with a hands-on-the-hips pose and a look of disdain. . . . Their voices are hostile and their questions reveal an unmistakable self-righteousness. The blame comes pouring forth: 'Why don't you men ever want to make a commitment?!' 'Why are you men only interested in sex?!' "[5]

Today, women are continually fed the line that we have to wrestle for control of our own life in order to be free, to be happy and to be fulfilled. Such tragedies as the vast increase in abortions stem from a woman's desire to make all the ultimate decisions for her own life. The term for those who favor abortion—pro-choice—symbolizes the right to choose, to be in control. *But at what cost*—to life, to human dignity, to a woman's personhood? Unfortunately, many have found that to be in control does not bring the promised results. Instead, control has meant bondage to destructive emotions like anger, fear and shame—emotional bondages that exist even among Christian women.

The recent movie *Dad* is a poignant story of an elderly man who has lived in a fantasy world most of his life—his way of coping with a controlling, domineering wife. When she becomes ill and goes into the hospital, he has to step out of the passive role he has adopted over the years and begin to do all those things he let her do for him. When his wife comes home, she finds his new, assertive role upsetting and insists that she wants her "old" husband back. What she is really saying is that she wants to be in control again. When she finds out about his fantasy life, she asks him: "Was it that difficult living with me?" He answers, "Well, you just took over, and I let you. You were so good."

## Let's Clarify As We Begin

This book is not written to blame women. The truth is, women *are* good at what they do. They have tremendous skills, gifts, abilities, and strengths.

[4]Ibid., p. 133.
[5]Ibid., pp. 133–134.

Yes, women *are* more sensitive and intuitive than men, and often grasp what needs to be done before a man will. And it is also true that some of us are "skilled" at taking control—either subtly, or overtly—and some men are skilled at letting us do it! The problem is, being in control is a human way of feeling secure, getting problems "solved," getting things done "right." But God has called us not to control but to a life of trust and ever-increasing faith, free of debilitating emotions and out-of-balance relationships.

A fair warning: Though my aims are to help us all find freedom, healing, and a new level of faith, some of what we discuss in the following chapters may cause discomfort.

Someone has said, "Truth is always negative in its first apprehension." I urge you to "hang in there" if the Holy Spirit brings to light glimpses of yourself that make you uncomfortable. He is both a cleansing fire *and* a gentle teacher.

Another temptation is to say that it's someone *else* who should change: a husband, son or daughter, mother or father, pastor, friend. We know, however, that only by the grace of God can we change ourselves. Ultimately, trying to take control over another person is to assume the place of God. When you and I do this, we have fallen into a most dangerous trap.

Another clarification I need to make: There are some women who are struggling under the weight of a dysfunctional authority over them. It may be a husband on drugs or alcohol, one who is flirting with sexual sin, or one who is mismanaging the family's finances for selfish reasons. It is possible, in these cases, that a woman can break through the deception that clouds her husband's inner vision by staging what is called an *intervention*, forcing him to face up to the truth of what he is doing to destroy his life and hers and the lives of their children. This type of "taking control" may be necessary and can be used by God to turn a man back to health and the truth. When it comes to moral and illegal lapses, I am personally in favor of this kind of intervention.

Mainly, though, I am talking to those of us who simply have not been able to let go and *trust*. Somehow we have taken the burden of our world—extended family, friends, Christian leaders, husband and children—upon our own shoulders. We *mean* well. We mean to fix things, and fix people. We want to keep our husbands on track. We want to keep our children from making mistakes and getting hurt. We want to keep our friends healthy and happy. And we want to keep our spiritual leaders wise. But we're not always clear as to what is best for these many folks we care about, whose well-being so greatly affects our own peace of mind—and so we improvise. We often make the mistake of believing that our will for them must be their highest good. (How could it be anything but?) And that is where *we* begin to go amiss, to lose our own peace—and to cause unhappiness and conflict for others. We have all seen—at least I know I have—how our best intentions can go astray. So I'm writing to encourage you: There are ways out of the control trap!

## A "True Confession"

I myself was a very insecure, controlling person for much of my life. I am more liberated today than I have ever been—but not in the sense that the feminists espouse. My liberation has been from fear, worry and insecurity into a wonderful new joy as I learn to trust my heavenly Father—and trust "my world" into *His* control. I have shared the principles in this book in countless counseling sessions and have seen them bring health and renewed relationships for many women. We will look at many aspects of this need to control, including:

- how we fall into the "control trap"
- how we take on the role of "director" at home
- the difference between pushing God and obeying Him
- the direct and indirect ways we control
- how fear is a type of control
- the three prongs of a woman's anger
- how to release control of your finances
- how to release your children to God
- the power that a woman has over a man
- God's view of control

Best of all, you will read the true experiences of women who are discovering how to relax in the arms of a faithful God who will never disappoint you—if you give Him full charge of your life.

For many of us, the invitation to *relax* may come as the most welcome word of all. It is God's invitation to you, as you read on.

*The wise woman builds her house, but with her own hands the foolish one tears hers down.*

*Proverbs 14:1*

# 2

# "But I Meant Well"

Why is it that a well-meaning person can sometimes find herself in such a mess? Some women find themselves accused of "abuses" and "crimes" they have no idea they committed. If this has happened to you, you know the result: *You* are left feeling worn, weary and unappreciated for all your hard work for others. After all, you *meant* well!

One story from history speaks of a woman who suffered incredible accusations and an even greater tragedy than you or I will ever know—all because of her well-intended efforts to control situations that were beyond her power. Her name was Alexandra, and she was the wife of Nicholas II, the last tsar of Russia.

## Portrait of a "Controlling Woman"

The story of *Nicholas and Alexandra*[1] is an intense and tragic drama set against a background of Russia's luxurious palaces, in contrast with a disgruntled peasantry and political unrest. Unknowingly, the empress—beautiful, loving Princess Alix with red-gold hair—steered her family toward disaster. A devoted wife and mother of five children, she was also fiercely dedicated to the welfare of her adopted Russia. All of this makes her tragedy more ironic—and full of urgent mes-

---

[1]Robert K. Massie, *Nicholas and Alexandra* (New York: Dell Publishing Co., Inc., 1967).

19

sages for those of us who worry over the fortunes of our lesser "ships of state."

The Tsar Nicholas was physically and psychologically like his mother: gentle, kind and slight of stature, the opposite of his enormous, harsh, overbearing father, the Tsar Alexander. Like many first sons, Nicholas bonded to his mother and she became his emotional support, acting as a buffer between son and father. Nicholas was so dominated by his father that at the age of twenty-five he could not marry the woman of his choice—Princess Alix of Hesse-Darmstadt—because his father would not approve his marrying a "hated German." Only when Alexander became suddenly and seriously ill did he relent and give his consent to the marriage.

There are uncanny parallels between the two most important women in Nicholas's life: Both his wife and his mother were charming and warmhearted women; both acted as buffers; and both were stronger internally than the gentle, kind, open-faced Nicholas.

As a boy, Nicholas turned to his mother for support and protection, so when his powerful father suddenly died, it was natural to turn for advice and counsel to his capable wife. Nicholas shrank from the domineering nature of his father, but succumbed to another kind of domination—the sweet and over-protective direction first of his mother and then of his Alexandra.

Alexandra, for her part, had gone through a painful experience in her childhood, which became a defining moment in her character. When Alix was six, her mother died and Alix was never the same. Afterward, "a hard shell of aloofness formed over her emotions, and her radiant smile appeared infrequently. She grew to dislike unfamiliar places and to avoid unfamiliar people."[2]

The trauma of her beloved mother's unexpected death caused Alexandra to pull inward and try to gain control—first, over her inner world of emotions; later, as empress, she extended that control to her home and even her nation as a way of guarding against more unexpected calamities.

When any one of us tries to form this kind of secure, protective shell, we immediately run up against people and circumstances that threaten the shell we have built. Alexandra's

---

[2]Ibid., p. 30.

first challenge was motherhood.

Her greatest desire was to give Nicholas a male heir to his throne. The Russian crown no longer passed down through the female line, so if Alexandra could not produce a son, the throne would pass to Nicholas's younger brother. "Over the next ten years, she had four daughters, each healthy, charming and loved, but still not an heir to the throne."[3]

For a strong woman like Alexandra, the thought of losing the throne was inconceivable. She prayed fervently for a boy. Finally, in 1904, her son Alexis was born. She was sure God had answered her ardent prayers.

But once again circumstances slipped out of her grasp. At six weeks of age, little Alexis suffered his first hemorrhage. Since Alexandra was a granddaughter of England's Queen Victoria, she was familiar with hemophilia, rampant in that royal family. What she feared was quickly confirmed. Russia's next tsar would be a feeble hemophiliac.

Alexandra suffered tremendous guilt, knowing that she had been the carrier of this dread disease now afflicting her son. As he grew, she agonized as the boy suffered again and again, hemorrhaging into a joint and screaming out at the pounding pain: "Mama, help me, help me!" To Alexandra, sitting beside him and unable to help, each cry seemed like a "sword thrust into her heart."[4] If only she could *do* something—particularly when his suffering was "her fault." Naturally, any mother would "cut off her right arm" to save her child, but for Alexandra it became one more piece of the control puzzle.

The overpowering guilt along with her genuine concern for her son's pain drove her to try to find a solution. She threw herself into the Russian Orthodox Church that openly believed in miracles and divine healing. She established a small chapel for her own use and spent hours on her knees praying for the cure of her son. As the years passed, however, her prayers went unanswered. She felt that God would not listen to her petitions. Why was He so cold and unfeeling? After all, hadn't He also taken away her mother?

Disappointment with God, as characterized by Philip Yancey, is another factor, like guilt, that causes some of us to seize

[3]Ibid., p. 152.
[4]Ibid., p. 153.

control of a situation. If God will not do it, then it is up to us. However, when we take this position, we open ourselves up to believing the lie that God is not faithful, that He cannot be trusted. For all our spiritual performance—prayer, Bible study, what have you—we have inwardly placed ourselves on the far side of a great spiritual chasm from God, carrying within us a gulf of hidden anger that separates us from the only source of life itself.[5]

When Alexis was eight years old he suffered a severe hemorrhage in the thigh and groin. For eleven days and nights he suffered so intensely the household servants stuffed cotton in their ears to drown out his screams. Alexandra scarcely left his bedside. With no other hope left, the priests administered the last rites. Alexandra frantically telegraphed Rasputin, the Siberian peasant-monk who was reported to have miraculous powers of faith healing. He immediately cabled back that he would pray and her son would live.

A day later the hemorrhage stopped. From that moment, "Alexandra was unshakably convinced that her son's life lay in Rasputin's hands. From this belief, enormous consequences were to flow."[6] Greater deception was taking hold. How many times do we, in the interest of controlling not only a problem but God himself, resort to the latest "faith formula" in an attempt to get Him to do our will? This question I have shuddered over too many times.

Rasputin was a controversial figure, to say the least, in St. Petersburg. He was filthy, a totally immoral man, a drunkard who seduced young women who came to talk to the "holy man." Nevertheless, he was hailed a miracle worker, some attributing it to his "hypnotic eyes." It is generally believed that Rasputin even used these extraordinary eyes to hypnotize the Tsarevich, giving hypnotic suggestions that caused the bleeding to stop. The empress never saw the evil side of Rasputin. She saw only a humble, saintly man in whose hands lay the power of life and death. When Alexandra accepted the lie that God did not care about her son's suffering, she was open to accepting other "spiritual" answers to her problem.

It is true that many women have spiritual capacities that make them sensitive to God. The number of grandmothers and

---

[5]For further reading, I recommend *The Hidden Rift With God* by William Backus, Bethany House Publishers.
[6]Massie, pp. 188–189.

mothers who have "prayed souls into God's kingdom" only eternity will reveal. But Alexandra's "spiritual sensitivity" overruled all the misgivings she may have had about Rasputin—to the detriment of her own husband's power to govern.

The "problem" of Rasputin became a public concern. He was known to have tremendous influence over the empress, and she in turn over the tsar. Since censorship had been abolished in Russia, "the press began to speak openly of Rasputin as a sinister adventurer who controlled appointments in the Church and had the ear of the empress. Newspapers began to print accusations and confessions from Rasputin's victims and the cries of anguished mothers."[7] He was publicly denounced by a Moscow newspaper, and tabloid-type papers printed the latest gossip. It was rumored that the empress was Rasputin's mistress and that he had raped all the young grand duchesses. Obscene chalk drawings appeared on the walls of buildings depicting Rasputin and the empress and he was the subject of smutty rhymes.

Throughout these attacks, the empress staunchly defended him. She urged her uneasy husband to dismiss government ministers and church bishops alike when they leveled accusations at Rasputin. She was not only fighting for the life of Rasputin, she was fighting for the life of her son and only heir. In her mind, she was also fighting for the future of the nation. She believed that she and Rasputin controlled the destiny of her family, and also the nation. Everything rested on her shoulders. Why wouldn't the rest of the world see things her way?

The situation was further complicated when Russia became involved in World War I against Germany. The Russian army suffered severe losses and was on the verge of collapse in 1915. At Alexandra's strong urging, the tsar took personal command of the army. "By going to the army, hundreds of miles from the seat of government, the Tsar gave up all but a vague, supervisory control over affairs of state. In an autocracy, this arrangement was impossible; a substitute autocrat had to be found. Uncertainly at first, then with growing self-confidence, this role was filled by the Empress Alexandra. At her shoulder, his 'prayers arising day and night,' stood her

---

[7]Ibid., p. 229.

'friend,' Rasputin. Together they would finally bring down the Russian Empire."[8]

Even when Rasputin was assassinated, the empress refused to release her control of the government. Many pleaded with her, including her brother-in-law: "You have a beautiful family of children, why can you not . . . please, Alix, leave the cares of state to your husband?"[9]

We may wonder why Alexandra did not respond to the pleas of those around her, but I am convinced she could not see that she had moved beyond the boundaries of her ability or that she had stepped into a place of authority that was not hers to take. She only wanted to do what was "best," sincerely believing that she knew what that was. She believed, therefore, that her heart attitude was right, and so she could use any means to achieve her goal.

Hatred and opposition grew against the empress. But the factor that contributed most to her defeat was the passiveness of her husband. Since the empress was German, the people began to feel she was secretly aligned with Germany and deciding issues that would bring defeat to Russia. Still the tsar refused to stop her, even when his closest friends pleaded with him. The president of the Russian imperial parliament passionately argued, "To save your family, Your Majesty ought to find some way of preventing the empress from exercising any influence on politics."[10]

Nicholas was, indeed, a passive man. He had allowed his wife to slowly erode his authority until, perhaps, he welcomed the chance to get away to the war front and leave the day-to-day responsibilities to her. He loved her deeply and his gentle nature kept him from taking a strong position of authority in her life. The more determined and aggressive she became, the more he withdrew. Like many men, Nicholas wanted peace at any price—but what a price he had to pay!

Finally, the tsar abdicated his throne in favor of his younger brother Michael. It was too late. The revolution exploded around them. On July 16, 1918, just eight days before their rescuers arrived in Sverdlovsk to free them, the tsar, the empress, and their five children were executed.

Perhaps Alexandra does not fit our mental image of a con-

---

[8]Ibid., p. 322.
[9]Ibid., p. 386.
[10]Ibid., p. 393.

trolling woman. She was not loud-mouthed, angrily denouncing "male chauvinism." But an outwardly aggressive, domineering "women's libber" is not the only portrait that can be painted of a controlling woman. Alexandra was a genteel, loving woman, deeply devoted to her husband and family. She and Nicholas continued to write each other love letters all during their marriage whenever they were separated, and it is on the basis of these touching letters that we can reconstruct this time in history.

## Your Heart Condition

Every woman who has a tendency to control is *not* a scheming Jezebel. I know that and, much more importantly, God knows that. So when He sheds His light within our hearts it is not the spotlight of cold, harsh, relentless "truth"—rather, it is the guiding light of His Holy Spirit, leading us out through dark, gloomy corridors of the soul to the open air. He leads us out from "control" to surrender and rest. He wants to help us recognize the prisons we have built around ourselves and come to the One who holds the key to freedom.

There are lessons we can learn from the life of a woman like Alexandra—and questions we must ask ourselves. The ones that follow may put the key to freedom within your grasp. You may want to take time to be alone and consider these questions.

1. *When circumstances are out of my control, or when people are doing things I don't like, do I sense something rising up inside, wanting to "take hold" of the situation and make it "come out right?" If so, do I mentally rifle through all the options until I find a "solution"?*

At times, when I take stock of the ways I have run out ahead of God, pushing to get things done "the right way" (or is it just *my* way?) I am mortified. Rather than wallowing in self-pitying thoughts about what a "terrible Christian" I am, I remind myself to stop leaning on my own understanding of circumstances and people, to turn from seeking my own way, to quiet my anxious spirit, and listen for God's plan. (See Proverbs 3:5.)

2. *When things are not going my way, what is my first-line*

*emotional response? Fear? A sense of shame that "I must have done something wrong to bring on this problem"? Anger?*

The deep need to control often has an emotional root. In this book we will examine the emotions that cause us to fall into the control trap—fear, anger and shame. For now, consider whether or not you are willing to honestly face deeply rooted emotional needs that God wants to heal.

3. *Do I ever use "spiritual performance" to try to influence others' opinions of me? Or to influence the outcome of a certain situation?*

As Christians, we must be careful not to use so-called spirituality to pressure or influence other people into doing what we want. I must ask myself if I sometimes wrongly use phrases like: "I was praying about this situation, and God told me to tell you . . ." Or, do I expect spiritual leaders to value my opinion over that of others because of my faithful attendance, hours of service, and obvious spiritual insight?

God longs to have real intimacy with us—not to have robotic, spiritual performers. All our good works will be as filthy rags (Isaiah 64:6) if they flow out of our own desire for recognition or self-will and not from the compassionate heart of our living God, who works through humble men and women.

4. *Do I look for "new, improved spiritual formulas" that will give me more leverage with God—get Him to answer more of my prayers?*

Alexandra fell into a trap in this area. We can, too. This may be humbling, but take a quick inventory of your prayer life. Are most of your prayers in the form of telling God *what* He should do, *when* He should do it, and *whom* He should do it to? Do you pray "Get him!" prayers—or prayers for mercy? Do you advise God, or do you listen for His guidance?

5. *Do I ever hear myself say: "I guess it's all up to me. If I don't do it, it won't get done"?*

Yes, it's true that your husband, children, father, pastor or co-workers may be frustratingly passive. Maybe they don't perform as you wish they would, or shoulder important responsibilities. But is it more important to you to get a certain function accomplished at the expense of building healthy, cooperative relationships? Have you considered what price you will pay in the end, emotionally and physically, if you burn yourself out bearing the weight of your private world alone? If it's truly "all up to you," is it *worth* doing? Are you trying, for some reason, to prove to others or to yourself that you are strong, that you can handle things on your own?

6. *Do I sometimes/frequently overstep the bounds of my authority?*

Some of us were the kind of kids who frustrated our parents no end. Maybe you heard your mom or dad all too often say, "You never take *no* for an answer, do you?" Or, "Why did you go ahead and do that when I specifically told you not to?"

The Roman centurion (see Luke 7) recognized that even Jesus was not a "free agent," performing miracles randomly with no specific plan or order. He recognized that Jesus moved only under the authority of God, and therefore He had the ability to perform works of love, wonder and power.

For some of us, authority means "limitation," a force to figure our way around. What does it mean to you?

7. *Am I sometimes angry, sometimes relieved when others step back and let me do things my way?*

If you are like most women who tend to take control, you experience emotional confusion from time to time. Sometimes you're all too happy to have others clear the deck, let you roll up your sleeves and show what you can do. It feels good to all of us to have our skills and contributions recognized. But then there are times when you feel like you're out on a limb, holding a big bag full of responsibilities. If you ever feel that way, ask yourself honestly how you got into that position. Most of us are masters at contributing to our own inner turmoil. This is simply to help you see a little more clearly through the fog.

*Did* you climb out on that limb so that others could get a good look at how well you can climb? What are you going to do to get down from there now that it's getting uncomfortable?

# Section 2

# BECOMING "THE DIRECTOR"

*Charm is deceptive and beauty is fleeting; but a woman who fears the Lord is to be praised.*

*Proverbs 31:30*

# 3

# *In the Director's Seat*

Most women do not realize how much influence they can have in terms of directing the emotional and spiritual climate of the home. Understanding how this influence comes to be ours not only can contribute to the inner health and growth of our families but will help us to wisely use that influence as servants of the Lord.

Women can function as the "director" in a home in much the same way as a director in the control booth oversees the functioning of a TV or radio program. I have some familiarity with a control booth since hosting a one-hour morning talk show covering the greater Chicago area. Though listeners had no idea, a great deal of the show's direction and format was in the hands of the engineer/director who sat behind a glass partition, signaling me when to begin, when to break for a commercial and when to wrap it up. Sometimes his facial expressions alone—a big smile, or dismal shaking of his head—would let me know how the show was going. Even though it was my radio show, it could not have been produced without the technician in the control booth whose influence permeated all I did.

Every home has a "director," so to speak, someone who sets the predominant emotional and spiritual thermostat, according to how "hot" or "cold" he or she feels toward many things. In fact, this person's attitude affects *most* things—whether it is show of affection, how time and money are spent, "acceptable" and "unacceptable" friends, family vacations, and much more. This person may not be in control all the time and may also have "a good reason" for directing. My question is: How *often* do you find yourself in the director's seat? Maybe you're not even happy with the sense of responsibility you feel for directing and engineering things. But let's look at how we women come to take over the director's position, sometimes to our own detriment and the detriment of others.

## Setting the Emotional Thermostat

Jim was on his way home from work after a particularly grueling day. His boss had been on his back all afternoon about a project he should have completed the day before. As he progressed slowly through the rush hour traffic, Jim was mentally sitting in his big green recliner in front of the TV. Maybe after an evening of kicking back—with no pressure—he'd be able to face work again tomorrow.

As he pulled into the driveway of his small, red brick ranch home, Jim felt himself tensing a little. As he walked in the front door, he paused momentarily—maybe twenty seconds—to assess the emotional climate in the house. He could hear Mary clattering around in the kitchen and carrying on an animated conversation with Tommy. When Jim heard her laugh, he let out a long, slow, sigh of relief. It would be a good evening.

## Emotional Climate

Jim is not unusual. And whether or not he should *want* to just go home and sit in his green recliner is not the real issue here. Many men take immediate inventory of the emotional climate in the home when they return from work—as if they are holding up a mental finger to see which way the wind is blowing. If Jim had "heard" a certain kind of silence, felt a tension in the house, or seen a particular set expression on Mary's face, he would have entered more cautiously. Perhaps he would have just mumbled a quick hello and hurried to his big green chair to hide behind the newspaper in an effort to escape. In all likelihood Mary, like most controlling women, would have been disapproving and felt anger and rejection for what she would see as an attempt to avoid responsibility—

and escape from her. How is it that an event so common as coming home can become a factor that contributes to a woman's control in the home?

One reason for coming into the director's position is that many women naturally seek help, support, even sympathy for a rough time they've had. The husband is not the only one in the family who faces pressures. A woman faces them also, whether as homemaker or on a job outside the home. Women like to talk through their day, sharing events, emotions, details large and small. Because a woman's first response is often on an emotional level, she can inject emotions into the air almost before she knows she has done it. Women communicate *emotionally* more often than they realize.

Many men seek quiet and solitude to work through their thoughts and feelings, often seeking some "field of battle" (even if it's a golf course or racquetball court) to work out pent-up emotions. As husbands, they may not be ready to deal with the realities of an emotionally intimate relationship. Some men are so completely out of touch with their own emotions that they cannot deal with those of their wife. These men generally let their wives set the "thermostat" in the home. They will take it as normal, whether they shiver alone in a lounge chair under chilly conditions, or bask in the warmth of acceptance and understanding. To many men, this is simply "the way it is."

A question for thought: Would it really be so difficult to give your husband a little emotional space when he comes in the front door? I am not referring to the "total woman" approach to marriage. But if your husband has a bit of quiet, he is more likely to be open and communicative over dinner or a shared cup of coffee. In our illustration earlier, Mary's emotional needs were *real*; Jim's emotional needs (yes, they were emotional) were *real*. Finding common ground for meeting both takes work and time but certainly is worth the effort.

## Signals

A second reason a woman may find herself in the control booth is that people *do* look to her for emotional signals. Natural nurturers and approval-givers, mothers are children's first link with the world. Wives often are the gauge by which many husbands answer their own spoken or unspoken question: "How am I doing?"

Experts estimate that as much as eighty percent of all communication is nonverbal. The tiny baby eagerly searches his mother's face and soon learns to respond to her expressions of love, fear or rejection. The adult male continues to respond to a woman's facial expressions and body language. How many of us are really aware of what we silently tell each other much of the time? Because most of us are not, we sometimes find people reacting negatively to us and don't know why. It took the honesty of my son John to help me begin to see how much silent influence I unknowingly held.

One day John, who was twenty-three at the time, was having an argument with our youngest daughter, Kelly, seventeen. I thought Kelly was old enough to handle it, and I'd stay out of it. But I must have been thinking that John, as the older of the two, ought to be more understanding. Because suddenly John turned to me, and uncharacteristically commented, "I hate that look of yours."

"What look?" I asked, startled. I had thought I was doing an excellent job of being impartial, a neutral bystander.

"It's a look of *total disgust*," John replied. "You've done it to me since I was a little kid."

Honestly, until John said this I had never been consciously aware of using a facial expression to control his behavior. The minute he pointed it out, however, I recognized the truth. How often had he squirmed inside while I thought I was letting him handle things his way? In shock, I realized that the signal I was sending to him was: "I am totally disgusted with you and nothing you do is right." When I asked John if that was the message he received from "that look" he did not hesitate.

"That's *exactly* what I feel." He even admitted he found this look so upsetting that once when a girl he dated had the same look on her face, he ended their relationship immediately.

With deep remorse I thought back over all the times I was aware of trying to control his behavior—for the normal, necessary reasons a mother must control the actions of a growing, active child. When he was three, I had discovered that I could control his behavior with "that look." If we were at a friend's house and he was about to do something that would embarrass me, I would raise my eyebrows and shoot him a severe look that meant, "Stop it—*now!*" John responded well to this type of correction. Firstborns, it has been noted, often require adult approval. (Whereas Tom, our third-born, had to be physically restrained because looks meant nothing to him.)[1] I had used facial expressions so long to control John's behavior that I no longer realized that I did it.

I discussed this issue with a women's study group. I asked if they were aware of controlling through non-verbal signals. After the laughter quieted enough for me to be heard, we discussed various "techniques." The most popular by far was rolling the eyes back as a way of communicating—"I can't *believe* what you just did/said." Here is a brief list of other "signals":

- tightening the mouth to indicate disapproval
- looking down when the other person is saying or doing something you find embarrassing
- raising eyebrows as a warning not to proceed any further
- hunching the shoulders and turning the face away, meaning "You have offended me."
- a "pasted-on" smile, meaning "Please change the subject immediately."

Recent research into the workings of both the male and female brain indicates that women are better communicators than men.[2] From birth more sensitive to sounds, tones of voice, and intensity of expression, females are more adept at verbal and expressive cues than males, and soon learn to control situations through these cues. A man may raise his voice and pound his fist, but a woman need only give a withering look. A recent article on First Lady Barbara Bush makes an interesting observation: "Barbara will probably never sit in on Cabinet meetings *a la* Rosalynn Carter, but her raised eyebrow can often defeat a stack of position papers."[3]

In a marriage relationship, nonverbal signals can become quite refined. The woman in the "control booth" can send a signal clear across the room at the office Christmas party. Her husband, in the middle of an amusing story, sees her message

[1]Barbara Sullivan, *No Two Alike* (Old Tappan, New Jersey: Chosen Books, Fleming H. Revell Company, 1987).
[2]"Men vs. Women," *U.S. News & World Report* (Aug. 8, 1988), pp. 50–55.
[3]Margaret Carlson, "Barbara Bush, Down-to-Earth First Lady," *Reader's Digest* (April, 1989), pp. 83–87.

that says, "You look like a fool." He quickly winds up his story and is strangely quiet the rest of the evening. Or, if he decides to rebel against her—as he most likely rebelled against his mother when he was younger—he might get louder and more raucous and end up really looking foolish. My point is: Either way, she has communicated what she intended.

## The Indirect Method

Another reason many of us fall into the director's role is because of certain frustrating blocks set before us early in life. Many girls are taught in both subtle and overt ways from early childhood that if they want something it is not "ladylike" or polite to go the direct route—to directly state what they want. Boys are allowed to act more aggressively and be direct. In fact, "by the age of two, boys begin to show signs of greater aggressiveness,"[4] which many parents encourage, believing this will help them become healthy leaders.

A girl, on the other hand, is often encouraged to learn other ways to communicate her honest feelings. Many of us were "set up" to be controlling or manipulative because we understood it is bad to be labeled as a "strong woman." A parent reinforces this message when he or she does not discipline directly but uses manipulative techniques to control behavior.

When I was young, we lived next door to a family with eight children. If one of the children misbehaved their mother would affect a very sad expression and say, "You are making the angels in heaven cry because of what you are doing." The children, who really didn't care if the angels were crying, simply ignored her. Often, you may hear a grandparent or another care-giver say, "Your mother is going to be very upset if you do that," rather than indicating, "I don't want you to do that." People who feel powerless often try to control others by invoking the anger of those they perceive as stronger or having more influence. It's also used as a way to avoid undesirable confrontation.

If a woman is direct and aggressive, she is often labeled a shrew—or worse. Joan Collins played a controlling woman on the television show *Dynasty*. She was portrayed as cruel and heartless, a woman who used and then discarded men. But

---

4"Men vs. Women," op. cit.

years ago, when Mary Tyler Moore played the wife on the then-popular *Dick Van Dyke Show*, she also got her own way every time there was a dispute. The difference was that she did it in a cute, indirect manner, so the contrast between her character and Joan Collins' seems light-years apart. Actually they both sat in the director's seat—the differences were only outward. The message is clear: A woman who is direct is always a tigress, so remain indirect and "feminine."

## The Security Seekers

Probably the most common reason that women find themselves sitting in the director's chair is that they are by nature security-seekers and nest-builders. They sometimes mistakenly equate control with security. We erroneously reason: "If I can just get control over this aspect of my life I will feel secure." In truth, the more control we have, the more insecure we will tend to feel, because something inside tells us that we are ultimately becoming more *responsible*, as well, for the actions and outcomes we are influencing.

Control is an outgrowth of fear, insecurity and lack of self-esteem. The more anxious a woman is the more she wants to control and, conversely, the more secure a woman is the less likely she will need to control.

Anxiety today is so commonplace that researchers at the National Institute of Mental Health say it is the number-one mental health problem. According to a 1984 NIMH study, "An estimated 13.1 million Americans suffer anxiety disorders. . . ." The study also found that "for women anxiety is one of the most predominant problems. (The other is major depression.) At the core of anxiety is the sense that you don't have control. . . . If you think that you have lost control, that you are vulnerable to someone else's disapproval or rejection or ridicule, that's a red flag for anxiety. You're going to be continually geared up in an attempt to regain mastery and control—and your body will react to this constant state of anxiety."[5]

Anxiety and fear are fostered by the climate of the world we live in—a world that seems to have lost all its controls:

---

[5] Arlene Fischer, "What Is Your Body Trying to Tell You?" *Redbook* (March, 1987), pp. 89–91, 164.

Our children are not safe even in the schoolroom, the Tylenol caplet I take could be poisoned, I could be shot at while driving to work on the freeway, the Savings and Loan where I have my account could collapse, my husband could have an affair (statistics tell us that 70 percent of American married men are having an affair), my child could become addicted to drugs and alcohol as early as grade school, my daughter could become a teenage pregnancy statistic.

On a more personal level, women are bombarded by messages that say, "Be tough. Be aggressive. Have it all. And don't let anyone control you. Be the ruler of your own destiny. You have the right to *choose*." This is, of course, blatant humanism, even when it is disguised (as sadly it is) as gospel truth. There is only one Lord who sets the boundaries of our lives from beginning to end (see Acts 17:25–28; Hebrews 12:2; Revelation 21:6).

When we women, who set the emotional and spiritual climate of our home, grab the reins of control through anxiety, what happens? The answer is this: *Anxiety* becomes lord.

Another reason anxiety may seize us is that a woman is generally more inclined to respond to threats against her family. "In our modern, industrial society, after the lions and snakes have been killed, the elements of nature have been largely subdued, and material necessities are commonly assured, the greatest danger to the family is not physical, but emotional. And when the family is falling apart from within, nine times out of ten the woman is the one who responds by calling the clergy or counselor for help."[6]

Far too often the director's seat has been vacated by the man, and the woman fills in for him. When a man is threatened emotionally he tends to withdraw, but when a woman feels threatened she digs in her heels. Pierre Mornell in his book *Passive Men, Wild Women* talks about this pattern in a marriage relationship. "It was her husband's withdrawal that made her furious in the first place. So, more agitated, she comes back at him with greater demands for 'something he's not giving her.' This causes him to retreat further. She becomes hysterical. . . . He lapses into complete silence, total passivity. She goes wild. The battle escalates."[7]

---

[6]Gordon Dalbey, *Healing the Masculine Soul* (Waco, Texas: Word Books, 1988), p. 41.
[7]Pierre Mornell, *Passive Men, Wild Women* (New York: Ballantine Books, October, 1980), p. 3.

This is not to negate a sad reality: Some men have slipped into almost total passivity. As one woman angrily put it, "Trying to get my husband to do *anything* is like trying to push a rope up a hill." And this is just the problem: *Most men cannot be pushed to do something—especially by their wives.* The majority will retreat further and further, until the home or office or church—whatever the stage of conflict—is little more than a battlefield, uninhabitable by any man or woman seeking real intimacy. That is because duties, tasks, and behaviors have become more important than love, joy, peace, patience— or any of the other spiritual fruits that nurture a smooth, desirable relationship.

The final scene is the lone woman in the director's chair and her husband a tiny object in the distance. Again, not to say it is her fault—only to say that many of us wind up feeling bereft when we have no idea how things came to be this way.

An author, speaking for many of today's liberated women, said recently, "We are serious about our need to be powerful and to be seen as powerful." Equating *power* with *control*, women have moved into the director's seat in the family, the workplace and the church. But that position does not bring security, only more anxiety and fear, because linked to that position is tremendous responsibility and accountability.

Fortunately, many women are beginning to understand what has been lost in the attempt to be independent and in charge. We are discovering that true freedom has nothing at all to do with control and everything to do with emotional and spiritual freedom that comes only under the day-to-day lordship of Christ. He alone—not our husbands or anyone else— sets us free from fear. As Christian women, we really do want God's will for our lives. But we don't always know exactly what it is, or how to reverse the sweeping flood of fear that carries us away from the solid ground of faith and trust on which we long to stand.

We can step out of that current of unrest and begin to understand God's plan for our lives and His sovereignty over us and over those we love. Later in this book, we will look at God's interaction with us as we relate to others.

First, we need to consider a few questions to determine if certain behavior is slipping over into the category of "controlling" because of fear:

1. How do I respond to change? Does it threaten? Am I trying

to keep things running smoothly, or am I satisfied with the status quo?

2. In confrontations, do I always have to have the last word?
3. Do I usually feel weak and helpless?
4. Am I afraid to fly? Drive? Be home alone? Deal with male repairmen, salesmen, supervisors or leaders?
5. Do I struggle with unnamed fears?
6. When riding in the passenger's seat of a car, do I tend to give directions or push my foot to the floor in an attempt to stop the car?
7. Do I use manipulative techniques such as tears or blame or inferred guilt to get my own way?
8. Do I have a strong desire to maintain peaceful relations with others at work, home, church, or is it more important to me that things be done in the way that seems "right" to me?

Excluding the last question, if you answered yes to two or more, it is likely that you often use control techniques, perhaps without even knowing it.

*May the words of my mouth and the meditation of my heart be acceptable in your sight, O Lord.*

*Psalm 19:14*

# 4

# *It's Better to Be Direct*

Lil gunned the engine of her red convertible before turning off the ignition. She stepped out—crunching the small tea-rose bush beside the driveway, and slamming the door so hard that the agency sign in her car window rattled. She burst through the front door, flung her coat at the six-year-old who stood with mouth ajar, and gave the man of the house a familiar hug—which left the woman of the house with mouth ajar. As the bangles on her wrist clanged together, Lil unpacked her sales kit to prepare for the demonstration, singing in an off-key alto voice, "I've gotta be me!" When others criticize her bizarre behavior, her response is something like, "I just say and do what's on my mind, and if people don't like it, well that's their problem, isn't it?"

The truth is, many who are not quite as flamboyant or obvious as "Lil" are trying just as hard to be in control—maybe even more so because it isn't immediately perceived as control.

But those of us who identify with the "free-to-be-me" approach—whether we wave the flag or simply live it out—need to examine why we tell ourselves that we need to directly control things, people, events.

Perhaps in the quietness of your heart you tell yourself things like: "After all, it's my duty as a Christian mother to protect my children from serious mistakes by 'helping' them make the 'right' decision." "My pastor doesn't *really* understand the needs in this church, so I have an obligation to keep him informed and to give him progress reports." "I know my daughter-in-law would be happier if she could see how she sabotages her marriage to my son, and if I really love her I should tell her." "Since my husband doesn't have much motivation, he needs my little pep-talks to help him get on the stick." "I can't stand sneaky, manipulative, wallflower types— I'm going to take charge and I don't care who knows it!" And, maybe most difficult to deal with, "I do want the Lord to use me, don't I?"

Beneath these statements lie several suppositions—basic ways of looking at the world and your role in it.

One of them is: "I am responsible for the outcome of the lives around me." Women tend to think this way—even if it is ultimately incorrect thinking. We often assume that looking out for others is part of our role in life. From an early age, we were inclined toward nurturing and trained to be care-givers, especially if we had younger brothers and sisters. We identified with our mother as she cared for us, our siblings and father. The problem is we can take on too much responsibility for the lives of others and become direct controllers when we come to believe that "The only way to get something done right is to do it myself," or that "If I don't help someone make the right decision, do the right thing, go the right places, *who will?*"

Our motivation can be right—but our assumptions and methods can be all wrong. It is only natural and understandable to want the best for our husband, children, pastor, friends. But we may be shocked to see the way these people view our sincere attempts to be helpful and loving. Because our desire is right, we are often blinded to the direct control we exert, which is wrong.

A woman who bears the burden of direct control actually pays a personal price that goes beyond the negative reactions of those around her. At first, she can see only the rewards of being in the control booth and calling the shots. Things do get done, and some people do appreciate her efforts. The busy pastor may initially appreciate the woman who offers to help him get organized; the hurting, needy friend or sister may, at first, appreciate someone coming in and compassionately taking charge when she is low. The direct controller will have a sense of fulfillment as she sees her efforts bring the desired results.

As you may be discovering, however, the long-term result is far more negative. <u>There comes a time when people want or need to take charge of their own lives</u>. Beyond this point, he or she will begin to resist even the most loving "suggestions." Relationships with family and friends begin to disintegrate when the recipients of "help" feel themselves succumbing to an outside influence and try to free themselves. Conversely, a woman may succeed in controlling another's life, <u>but eventually she too will come to resent that person's</u> dependence on her. As a result, it can deteriorate into a love-hate relationship on both sides.

Another negative factor is that when we attempt to be the one in control of a relationship, we forego real intimacy with the other person because they are afraid to reveal weaknesses to us. (Doing so would only give us added power.) Our relationships, therefore, will most likely remain shallow and unfulfilling. Finally, the stress of being the controlling person, the responsible party, will eventually exact its toll on our bodies and we may suffer physical illnesses—all this, even though we set out with good motives.

If we are not talking about the "Lil's" of the world, then whom exactly *are* we talking about? Following are several portraits of direct controllers and some of their techniques.

## The Boss     *organized*

Caroline is the epitome of the happy, suburban housewife. She is thirty-nine years old, married to a successful businessman, and the mother of three children. She is a full-time wife and mother, active in her church and the PTA, and takes an aerobics class to stay in shape.

Caroline's oldest son, Charles, will leave for college next year, but it's not the happy "first flight from the nest" she hoped for as a Christian woman. They keep arguing over his choice of schools. She wants him to live at home for two years and attend the local junior college, but Chuck wants to go to a university in another state because of their excellent program in pharmacology. Caroline has bombarded Chuck with statistics about the advantages of staying home for the first two years of school. Their running argument has gone on for a full month. Caroline has even heard herself say—to her own dismay—"I don't think your father and I can get behind your plan financially. You'd better think about *that.*"

Caroline's husband conveniently sidesteps any involvement in the argument—as he always has. He works long hours and is content to leave problems on the home front in Caroline's very capable hands. Recently Caroline had to go to the hospital for a bleeding ulcer. Chuck is beginning to feel badly and wonders if his "rebellion" has caused his mother's problem.

Caroline has become an obvious controller—the boss—both because of her husband's lack of input and because of her own choice to "make things come out right."

A woman of Caroline's type is usually a very organized individual, and because she is competent she feels she has earned the right to manage everyone and everything around her. She has dominated her children's lives and has no reason to believe it will be or should be any different. Her security in life comes from being in control, so she rules her husband and her children, convinced she is doing what's best for them.

In Caroline's case, she didn't realize that Chuck's desire to go out-of-state to school was actually an attempt to escape her control. She also did not realize her bleeding ulcer might be connected with anxiety because of her reluctance to let go. Now both are miserable—Chuck feels guilty because of his resentment toward his mother, and Caroline is hurt that her son cannot see she wants only the best for him.

Maybe you can empathize with Caroline—if not in her methods, at least in her concern for someone she loves. She wanted her son to do what was "right" and thought she knew what "right" for him was. Caroline fell into the "control trap." Examining both her methods and the fruit of her efforts reveals this.

A woman's position in the family constellation is the first factor that has a significant impact on her *style* of controlling. In many cases, a firstborn girl is often given a large share of responsibility at home. In fact, a study found that firstborn girls did sixty percent more work than firstborn boys.[1] Caring

[1]Marion Long, "First Sons," *Chicago Sun Times*, Family Weekly (July 22, 1984), p. 14.

for younger siblings, she learns to "boss" and dominate in order to exercise her leadership. A firstborn girl seldom rebels against the overload of responsibility, but instead turns it inward and bears the consequences that can include physical suffering such as ulcers or migraine headaches.[2] She comes to believe early in life that the happiness and safety of others is dependent upon her. *youngest*

The youngest child also may become a "baby boss" and favor direct control methods. Noted psychologist Alfred Adler says that because the youngest child is for many years the smallest and weakest member of the household, he or she often sets out "to prove that he can do everything."[3]

A second reason a woman may fall into the "it's-all-up-to-me" trap is because something in the past has made her feel responsible to bear the load of family shame. This is especially true in the case of a dysfunctional family. She may have taken on the "hero" role or been a strong-willed child who learned to boss her family and get away with it because her parents were too dysfunctional or passive to notice or care.

Thirdly, even a woman's spiritual gifts can get out of balance and influence her method of control. For example, if she has the gift of mercy she will involve herself in others' suffering—especially if she thinks she can help them avoid it. But if she allows her own discomfort to control the situation, she is actually sparing herself. Even though she also wants those in difficulty to mature and stand on their own feet, she really wants to be spared the sorrow she will feel watching them struggle through the process. The bottom line is her motives can become selfish.

Perhaps her spiritual gifts may be in the area of organization and administration. She may be the kind who can play "mental chess" and figure out exactly what the outcome of a given situation will be, long before others even anticipate there is a problem. She has it "all worked out" by the time the rest are just waking up, and it's very natural to hand out assignments to everyone to keep things functioning smoothly. So shouldn't she use her gifts? Yes, but probably not as quickly as she might be inclined to do. Rushing to carry out her own

---

[2]Lucille K. Forer, *Birth Order and Life Roles* (Springfield, Ill.: Charles C. Thomas Publishers, 1969), p. 57.
[3]Alfred Adler, *Understanding Human Nature* (New York: Fawcett World Library, 1969), p. 123.

quick solution may cause her to miss a better solution from someone else.

Fourth, a woman may have to take responsibility because her husband is "not there" either physically or emotionally. A wife whose husband travels most of the week because of his job may feel forced into the position of boss. The question here, of course, is the fine line between guiding, nurturing and caring for her family, versus *controlling.*

Alexandra often chided Nicholas for his passivity and lack of authority. "Forgive me, precious one," she began to write in April 1915, "but you are too kind and gentle—sometimes a good loud voice can do wonders and a severe look. Do, my love, be more decided and sure of yourself."[4] Not too likely, given her predisposition to force it on him! It reminds me of a mother screaming at her children, "Now you stop screaming at each other!"

Former First Lady Nancy Reagan was criticized for being too domineering. Former White House Chief of Staff, Donald T. Regan, wrote in his memoir, *For the Record,* that Ronald Reagan was "immensely likable but disturbingly passive and vulnerable to manipulation." And he paints a surprisingly dark, mean-spirited First Lady, whose meddling became "the random factor in the Reagan presidency."[5] He notes how quickly she stepped in to protect "Ronnie" when she felt others were taking advantage of him. Whether or not these things are all true, it's easy to see how well-meaning behavior can be misinterpreted and even destroy a relationship we are attempting to strengthen. What is less easy to see sometimes—and less easy to face—is how a woman can slip into a mothering role. Beyond her direct responsibilities with her children, she can become "the mother" even to her husband.

## The Mother

Have you ever found yourself acting like your husband's mother—scolding him for tracking mud into the house or leaving his socks on the bedroom floor, excusing his behavior to friends and relatives, giving him lunch money from the family

---

[4]Robert K. Massie, *Nicholas and Alexandra* (New York, N.Y.: Dell Publishing Co., Inc., 1967), p. 330.
[5]Barrett Seaman, "Good Heavens!", *Time* (May 16, 1988), pp. 24–25.

budget, or nagging him because he forgot to wear a scarf on a cold day? The more a woman treats her husband like an incompetent little boy, the more likely he will behave like one—either rebelling against her or sliding into childlike dependence.

This pattern is evident in the relationship between Queen Jezebel and King Ahab of Bible times. Ahab wanted to own the vineyard of his neighbor, Naboth. When the man refused to sell, "Ahab went home, sullen and angry . . . He lay on his bed sulking and refused to eat" (1 Kings 21:4). In short, Ahab was acting like a young child having a temper tantrum. Jezebel, for her part, treated him more like an overprotective mother than a wife:

> Jezebel his wife said, "Is this how you act as king over Israel? Get up and eat! Cheer up. I'll get you the vineyard of Naboth the Jezreelite" (v. 7).

Jezebel reinforced Ahab's immature behavior by her action. Apparently she liked the role of the strong partner, the one in control, the capable mother-figure who could get her husband what he could not get for himself. Often, when a woman behaves like this, it is to show a man why he needs to depend on her. She may be seeking to prove to him that she is indispensable, that he cannot get along without her.

This "mothering" kind of control is easy to spot in a marriage relationship. It often begins very naturally, particularly after a woman becomes a mother for the first time. She is a mom all day, and it can be difficult to switch gears when her husband comes home from work. Eventually he can become another of her children, someone to manage, control.

In some cases the husband has set out to "replace" his own mother and purposely chooses a woman who will carry on the nurturing he craves. This can be an unhealthy situation for both partners in the marriage and may require prayer and counseling to arrive at a new level of commitment and trust.

One night my husband and I took a visiting speaker and his wife out for pie and coffee after the church service. While we were eating, the wife reached over and wiped a dab of banana cream pie off her husband's chin with her napkin. John and I smiled, and she said apologetically, "Sorry—I guess I don't get away from the kids too often."

As hard as it may be to switch gears, it is unwise and unhealthy not to make the effort. If we don't, the distinctive masculine and feminine roles peculiar to marriage are lost.

It is not uncommon to see older couples locked into this type of relationship: he—the sullen, pouting child who wants his own way; she—the strong, nurturing figure who will provide what he wants if only he will be a "good boy." But Barbara De Angelis, a marriage therapist, says that "behaving like a 'mommy' is the quickest way to kill passion in your marriage. After all, what man wants to sleep with his mother?"[6]

Often a woman who is married to a substance-abuser takes on the mothering role and becomes an unwitting "enabler." She cleans up, covers up, and makes up for him, enabling the substance-abuser to continue his addiction. She is the mother who scolds, punishes, and then accepts back her wayward child. Many times she feels frustrated and angry that she is powerless to change him—and therein lies the trap: *It is not up to her to change him*—(or to clean up for him, for that matter.)

Because she does not realize this, she can take on the responsibility for his behavior and suffer because of it. In addition, she may be the only one in the family earning an income, and so has the added burden of finances. But ultimately, as Dr. De Angelis states: "No man wants to feel that he is a woman's 'project.' "[7] When a woman takes on responsibility for a man's behavior, she subtly reinforces his irresponsibility.

Both the "boss" and the "mother" have a sincere desire to help—but the net effect is that they have seized direct control. The question is: Does her control really help? And what effect do her methods actually have on those she's controlling?

My husband and I have worked with substance-abusers for nine years. Though this book is written mainly for "average" couples, I think that a principle will be seen vividly in an extreme case.

One night, John and I were counseling the wife of a former drug addict about her pessimistic attitude toward her husband. She replied, "I can't really trust him yet. He'll have to prove himself." She wanted to help her husband and believed that withholding approval until he lived up to her expectations was the way to control his behavior and keep him from

---

[6]Barbara De Angelis, *Secrets About Men Every Woman Should Know* (New York: Delacotre Press, 1990), p. 31.
[7]Ibid.

relapsing. Actually, her negative attitude gave him the excuse he needed to justify his behavior. He began to reason, "No one really believes I'm going to make it—not even my own wife—so I might as well just quit trying." Of course, in a very real sense this man is accountable for his own choices. But the point is that negative reinforcement, like enablement, provides an "out." A man who is working to overcome any negative behavior needs both *responsibility* and *encouragement*.

## The "Nag"—That Dreaded Word

Another technique that the direct controller can resort to is *nagging*. The word "nag" comes from the Scandinavian *nagga* and means to gnaw or chew repeatedly. When a woman nags her husband, children and others, it is as if she is gnawing on their souls, with devastating effect. She may in the short-term get what she is after, but it will be at the expense of long-term values. A story from Scripture illustrates this.

When we think of Delilah, we may picture a raven-haired beauty with seductive eyes luring Samson into her loving embrace. But Delilah was also a nag. The rulers of the Philistines asked Delilah to find out the secret of Samson's great strength and they would reward her with a large quantity of silver. Delilah tried to find out three times, and each time Samson tricked her. Finally, in exasperation, she began to berate him:

> How can you say, "I love you," when you won't confide in me? This is the third time you have made a fool of me and haven't told me the secret of your great strength. *With such nagging* she prodded him day after day until he was tired to death. So, he told her everything. (Judges 16:15–17, italics added)

Delilah's nagging finally got to Samson and he broke his vow and told her his secret. He went to sleep in her lap and when he awoke his hair was gone and so was his unusual power. Her nagging eventually robbed Samson of his strength, his masculinity—and his life.

In a similar way, nagging can strip spiritually and emotionally the inner strength and identity of the one being berated. A man may feel emasculated; a child may lose his/her ability to set goals and achieve; others not so close may simply retreat from the barrage and the sense of losing power over their own souls.

The direct controller who nags in the attempt to gain total submission and excessive accountability will quickly drive people away. Probably the most irritating and recognizable controller, the nagger, will find her husband tuning her out, withdrawing from her, avoiding intimacy, finding a hobby, working long hours, or using myriad other ways to resist her demands or even sabotage her. Children will become rebellious in an attempt to defend themselves. A pastor or other Christian leader will go out of his way to avoid encounters with her. Even the best of friends will tire of interference in their lives and move on to freer relationships. As overt as nagging seems to everyone else, you may need to listen to yourself for a while to recognize this bad habit in your own life.

## The Intimidator

Another technique a woman may use to directly control is intimidation. To intimidate, according to the dictionary, is "to inspire with fear; to overawe or cow, especially with a forceful personality." An intimidator is like a simmering pot always ready to boil over. If even slightly provoked, her anger flashes a warning signal. People learn to tiptoe around so as not to "upset" her. In this way, she keeps herself constantly at the center, in full control, because everyone is trained to glance her way to see how she is reacting.

I was once the guest in a home where the woman clearly controlled by intimidation. As we sat around the table after dinner, I noticed that every time one of the children or the husband said anything, they'd quickly glance at Mother to see how it was affecting her. If she seemed pleased with what was said, the person would relax. But if she got a pouty look on her face, as she frequently did, the person responded as if slapped in the face. They would even stop telling a story or incident mid-sentence—perhaps fearing the consequence after the guest was gone.

It is stressful for all concerned to live under this type of control. Those intimidated may bury their anger, but it will surface in others ways. As mentioned previously, a husband may lose all interest in intimacy with his wife, in this case a passive/aggressive way of dealing with his anger. He may become secretive to avoid her wrath. He may even have an affair as a means of getting even. Children may become "forgetful" about the things that Mom asks them to do. They too may want to get even.

However it is discovered, when we find ourselves in the trap of the direct controller we need to escape—*quickly*. Otherwise, the ultimate end will be pain, broken relationships and overwhelming guilt. But *how* can one escape attitudes and actions that may have become a way of life? Habits of thinking and reacting that have been developed into an "art form" over many years?

First, we need to submit to God's plan, not only for our own life but for our husband, children and others around us. We must acknowledge our control and then relinquish it to God. A prayer that I often pray when I don't know God's will for a particular day is that God be glorified in the life of my son, daughter, friend, husband. It is a perfect prayer, Jesus' prayer before He went to the cross (John 12:28). It helps me to consider whether I am really submitted to God's plan.

We can also ask the Holy Spirit to give us a quiet spirit and help us keep a tight rein on our tongue (Psalm 141:3). If you are like me, you may have to pray this many times throughout the day.

You may also need to go to someone and ask their forgiveness. We must let others know when we recognize we have been controlling and do want to change. Tell them that you are returning authority to God. Though you will continue to pray for God's best for them, you will no longer make the decision as to what that best is.

If they have been under your control long enough, the sudden shift may be an adjustment for them, and you will need to decide with them the limits of your "advice-giving."

When another person mentions a problem or situation, you could say: "Are you asking for advice? Or would you just like me to be a 'sounding board' so you can think this through yourself?" We need to allow others to mature at their own pace and even make mistakes. They will then know that we support them, love them, and pray for them no matter what.

Once John and I counseled a couple to postpone their wedding for a period of time. We felt they weren't mature enough to take on the responsibility of marriage. We assured them, however, that we would continue to talk with them and encourage them no matter what their decision. They did decide to go ahead with the wedding as planned, and John graciously performed the ceremony. And our promise of support left the door open for further discussion and help when the going got rough. They did have many problems because of their immaturity, but our commitment was to help them overcome the problems and establish a strong marriage—not prove we were right. As a result, they felt the freedom to ask for help, and have gradually built a stronger home.

Remember, even though others don't necessarily do things our way, we can continue to encourage them rather than give "cautions" and veiled threats or hints of destruction. "Don't come crawling back to me to fix things up when you've blown it," is not the attitude to take. Leave the welcome mat out.

Finally, repent and confess if you find yourself back in the control trap. Breaking old habits takes time. Be patient with yourself—but diligent.

The obviously direct controller, "Lil," may be rude, overbearing and dogmatic, and she makes no apology for it. Although we all recognize a mother, mother-in-law or friend (never ourselves!), who may be a direct controller, most of us are much more subtle in the ways that we control. Most women have a tremendous fear of being *viewed* as aggressive or controlling, feeling it is the very antithesis of femininity. With this aversion to that image, most of us control in much more subtle and deceptive ways. And if we are successful, many of us will not even realize we are doing it.

In the next chapter we will consider the various indirect tactics of control.

*All the words of my mouth are just; none of them is crooked or perverse.*

*Proverbs 8:8*

# 5

## *It's Better to Be* Indirect

Lora drove cautiously up the driveway, careful to avoid the tricycle tipped over on its side. She took a deep breath before ringing the doorbell. She hated going to social gatherings without her husband, but he was away on a business trip and she had promised her old friends, the Harrisons, she would definitely attend their daughter's engagement party. She hoped the pale beige suit would be appropriate; but maybe she should have had her hair done, rather than pulling it back in its usual *chignon*.

When her friend Ginny opened the door, Lora quickly apologized. "Sorry, I'm a little early. I hope I haven't inconvenienced you. I promise I won't get in your way—maybe I can help out in the kitchen."

Ginny knew better than to argue, because she realized Lora would rather be "busy" than free to talk with other guests. When Lora attempted conversation, she was all agreement and smiles—but she had a hard time with eye contact. Eventually, her nervousness came through and made other people uneasy. *Yes*, Ginny thought, *she'll definitely do better in the kitchen.*

No one would suspect, even for a moment, that Lora is a controller. If anything, she's the type you'd urge to speak up for herself. Indirect controllers are hard to spot—precisely be-

57

cause their control does just that: it comes from any other direction than head-on. Indirect controllers usually feel they cannot get what they want by themselves, under their own strength. They feel weak, as if they have no power over their lives. To get what they want, they have to work through other people who are perceived as stronger and more capable, or they must rely on "socially acceptable" means of getting what they want.

By what reasoning does an indirect controller justify her methods? Here are a few in thought form; see if you can readily pick them out.

- I objected to several points in the pastor's sermon this morning—but if I mention it he might think I'm really petty. Maybe I'll just give him a book with the opposing viewpoint.
- I don't want to tell my husband I'm afraid to stay alone tonight, because he'll think I'm a baby. I'll just pretend I'm getting sick.
- I hate it when Sandy and her dad argue. I'm going to cook a special dinner tonight and maybe that will help to smooth things over.
- I need new carpeting for the Christmas party, but I know salesmen never pay attention to women. I'll tell him my husband insists we have the carpeting in three weeks.
- I know I'm under-paid, but I'm so thankful someone was willing to employ me. Maybe I could get Mary to suggest to the boss that I need a raise.
- I know I don't discipline the kids enough, but I'm so afraid they won't love me. Maybe I could ask their Sunday school teacher to say something to them about the need to be more obedient.

The problem of the indirect controller is that she feels inferior to others, so she feels she has little influence with them. As a result, she never issues a direct order or makes a straightforward request. She is convinced that, by herself, she is not capable of gaining control over her life. She uses people, situations, sickness, tears—*anything* but direct confrontation—to get what she wants. Most often, the things she wants are good things—companionship from her husband, peace in her family, a well-deserved raise, the best for her children—but the means used to achieve those ends can become manipulative and deceptive.

At first, it seems that indirect control does bring the desired rewards: We get what we want and, as a bonus, we're not viewed as aggressive and controlling. The indirect controller's main goal is to hide from others, and from herself, the fact that she is controlling. She learns to use others to get what she wants and deceives herself into thinking that she is too kindhearted to confront or too worried about the feelings of others, when in actuality she is too concerned with *appearing* kindhearted. She is motivated by a deep, self-protective desire.

But the long-term results of indirect control will produce bad fruit. Jesus said that a bad tree cannot produce good fruit (Matthew 7:18), and in the same way wrong methods, in the long-run, will not produce good results.

The first result from practicing indirect control is that we too may fall prey to the effects of deception. The woman who uses illness to elicit sympathy, for instance, can eventually become controlled by that ploy or by actual sickness. (Illness can be worked up in the imagination until we actually begin to feel ill.) Or, in the case of real illness, the constant use of the illness as an excuse for everything becomes a habit that clouds the motives.

Indirect control sends a double message and can produce double-minded children who could develop a love/hate relationship with us. This is because indirect control plays on another's guilt in order to get them to do things for us, and consequently cancels out true relationships based on honesty and trust. A child is naturally trusting and open-minded. If they detect that we are not completely up-front about what we are doing or asking them to do, they can become confused and feel they don't know us as we really are.

In the final analysis, indirect control may be more detrimental than direct control because the problem is more easily recognized in the case of direct control. Indirect control sends up a smoke screen to disguise true motives, creating confusion and frustration, and eventually even hatred.

## The Manipulator

Betty has always been a quiet, retiring little mouse. Her shoulders slump with the defeated look of a woman who has given up on life. When Betty's husband, Herb, leaves for a week of sales calls, she stands at the door, sad-faced, watching him go. Herb remembers the look on her face all week long and feels inwardly torn by the guilt of leaving her and the need to earn a living. When he calls home, she always spends the time telling him of the difficulties she's having. Of course she's quick to add, "I know you've got enough on your mind. I hate to bother you with my troubles."

Betty never verbally asks her only child, Angela, to stay home and keep her company when Herb is gone. But when Angela mentions going out, Betty gets a frightened look on her face and says, "Oh, don't worry about me, I'll be okay. You have a good time."

If Betty doesn't like a young man her daughter is dating, she never tells Angela how she feels but makes remarks like, "You know, John seems like a nice young man—but he doesn't have much ambition, does he?"

Betty would never disagree with her husband's decisions directly. Rather, she agrees with him at the time, but later offers comments of her own, such as, "Do you really think that's a good idea?" or, "I've been thinking about what you said and wondered if. . . ?" Herb then begins to second-guess his decision.

When you find yourself getting upset with a woman like Betty, *you* feel guilty. This is because the person who just manipulated you seems to be so sweet and kind. You wonder, *How could I be upset with her? I must be a very uncaring person.*

In contrast, the *direct controller* plays on a person's insecurities. She presents herself as stronger and more knowledgeable and her overbearing manner is intended to intimidate. To go against her demands will require an argument on your part, and so it is often easier to take a passive role. But the *indirect controller* plays on your guilt feelings. *She* takes the passive role, and by manipulation gets you to offer to do something you really don't want to do. You end up angry and confused.

If Angela canceled her plans to go out and stayed home with her mother, Betty would have insisted that she really wanted Angela to go out and have a good time. Even though it was Angela's decision, she would feel "used" without understanding why she felt that way.

Betty really believes her own deception that she is a helpless, totally ineffective person. Herb and Angela will end up hating her control over them, but most likely will be unable to see it clearly enough to do something about it. Betty herself hates the fact that she is dependent on others and feels at their mercy. She uses all kinds of manipulative ploys, and when one tactic no longer works she switches to something else. She is tormented by the fear that those close to her will leave her.

Although Betty is a somewhat extreme example, most of us can probably relate to the indirect method of control—particularly if used "only occasionally" for "a good reason."

Why do so many women, even we Christian women who want the truth to set us free, fall into the trap of being indirect controllers? As with direct controllers, our family birth position influences our style of control. Second children, especially, learn to be great negotiators and manipulators. They often feel they cannot go the direct route to their parents, like the firstborn sibling who appears to have more "status" and credibility with parents, so they learn to "run plays around the end instead of bucking the line."[1] In fact, most later-born children prefer indirect control. An only child often feels helpless because she spends her entire childhood among adults whose abilities are far superior to hers.[2] This situation would produce a dependent person who feels she has to count on others to get what she wants.

Other *natural* factors may also apply. For instance, a girl may have had a more passive personality while very young, and others easily dominated her. Or she may come from a male-dominated home, where being *female* was equated with needing to be "protected." In a male-dominant culture, a man loses face if he does not rule his home. The women in such an environment learn to get what they want in a compliant, non-threatening way that allows the men to continue to believe they are in charge.

A woman may also learn indirect control when other factors, goals or people are generally thought to be more important than her needs. For instance, in a traditional marriage where the woman remains in the home as a housewife, her needs may be perceived as less important than those of her

[1]Lucille Forer, *The Birth Order Factor* (New York: David McKay Co., Inc., 1976), p. 53.
[2]Rudolf Dreikurs, *The Challenge of Parenthood* (New York: Hawthorn Books, Inc., 1958), p. 47.

husband, whose role as the breadwinner seems to have more importance. Whenever the needs of one member of a family are given greater priority, the others will tend to feel inferior. This can occur in the case of one member having a debilitating illness, or when one is unusually successful, or after the death of a family member. Whenever members of a family cater to one person for whatever reason, it is easy to perceive themselves as second-class citizens.

Many indirect controllers come from shame-based families, that is, homes where blame is consistently placed on a family member or on the whole family because of an addiction, a disability, or financial or social status. Although a woman naturally has wants and needs, she has been led to believe that her wants and needs are not as important as those of others in the family. Therefore, in order to get what she wants, she has to be manipulative, convincing all concerned, including herself, she didn't really bring it about on her own. Because she feels worthless, she believes she doesn't deserve to have things turn out for her benefit.

Control, direct or indirect, and regardless of whether we recognize it, will eventually harm our relationships.

What are some of the tactics of the indirect controller, and what effect does her control have on others?

## The Martyr

The martyr is usually a very self-sacrificing wife and mother. She may also be the enabler in an addictive relationship. She is almost too good to be real. And that is exactly the case.

Mary's brother is getting married next Saturday and Mary still doesn't have a dress to wear. Her husband encouraged her to buy a new dress over a month ago, but the money set aside for it was frittered away as Mary spent it on the children's needs.

Lisa, her eighth-grader, came home from school one day and announced she had to have a pair of the latest designer jeans. "*Everyone* will be wearing them to the spring picnic," she wheedled. So Mary took some of her dress money to buy the jeans for Lisa. The rest of the money went to buy Todd, her fifth-grader, shoes for Little League.

Often, when Mary drives Todd to his games, she comments

on his new shoes and how glad she is that she could buy them. Mary finds opportunities to assure Todd and Lisa that she didn't really want a new dress anyway. "My old blue one is good enough," she insists.

At the wedding, Lisa and Todd feel vaguely guilty as they notice how old and familiar their mother's dress looks. Lisa determines to be extra nice to her mother, hoping to make up to her for buying the jeans. Secretly, Lisa feels that she must be a very selfish girl, and wonders if she will ever be as self-sacrificing a wife and mother when she gets married.

The martyr controls through guilt and obligation. Her family and friends reason: "After all she's done for me, I owe her something." The martyr is always in a superior position— that of giving and sacrificing. Those on the receiving end— friends, husband or children—are left feeling selfish and self-centered. The martyr can give but is unable to receive. Receiving would mean losing her superior position, so she protests, "Oh, you spent too much money on me! I'm going to return it." Or, "No, I don't need any help today. I'm sure you have better things to do." Or, "You go on without me, I don't want to spoil your fun."

Like all controlling women, the martyr suffers from a very poor self-image. She attempts to strengthen her self-image by assuming the "super-good" role in a relationship. Hard as she may try to resist, she develops a strong spirit of pride through her constant self-sacrifice. The more selfish and self-centered others become, the greater her sense of pride. She controls through her service: Others owe her so much that they cannot break away from her.

Diana's father died when she was ten years old. She always thought there had to be something she could have done to prevent his death. This type of "magical" thinking is common among children, but because it was not dealt with Diana continued to carry this guilt into adulthood. She married a brilliant but unstable man who was unable to hold a job. Consequently, Diana held two jobs for the next twenty years, keeping the family together. She found herself alternating between loving and hating her husband. Over the years she also found that any attempt he made to stabilize his life brought a surprising response from her. She would say things like, "I'm not sure you should go for that job interview now—after all, you've been out of the work force so long." And because she earned the money, he gradually allowed her to control the budget.

Diana's friends said she was a saint, but in reality Diana was controlling her family and her marriage through martyrdom. Beneath it all, she still felt she had to somehow make up for failing to protect her dad. By becoming the martyr in the marriage relationship, she was avoiding a similar trauma.

The woman who takes on the role of the martyr may sincerely desire to help others, but instead keeps them locked into immature behavior patterns. If she is always there to "do for them," they will never learn to do for themselves. Diana, meaning no harm, kept her husband immature and dependent upon her. She took away his initiative to do things on his own and ended up in control of the relationship.

## The Invalid

Some years ago, a favorite movie character was the matriarch of a family who got "palpitations" whenever a family member went against her wishes. Most women who control through illness are not so obvious, but many women have used a headache to indirectly control one or two situations in their life.

Rita appears to be a healthy, well-adjusted woman, but she is often afflicted with migraine headaches. Her family knows that all the plans she makes are tentative—if she gets one of her headaches she will be unable to carry them out.

She promised her husband Joe she would go to a retirement party at the end of the week for his best friend. Joe knew the likelihood of Rita breaking her promise, but he hoped for the best. All week he helped out around the house to make things easier for her. Then on the day of the party, Rita came down with a bad migraine and was unable to go. Joe felt guilty because Rita was sure her headache was caused by the solvent he used in the basement to clean his tools.

Rita's children know they need to be very quiet around the house when Mom has one of her headaches. Dad is constantly warning them, "Don't have the TV on too loudly—Mom has a headache." Or, "No, you can't have anyone in to play today. You know your mother's in bed." Or, "Make sure you kids mind your mother today and don't give her any trouble. She doesn't feel well." When Rita wants the children to help her clean up the house, she simply rubs her forehead and mentions that she would do it if she wasn't so exhausted. Besides, helping them with their homework has given her the headache.

Maggie, her oldest daughter, often stays home from school to care for her mother. Sometimes Maggie is angry because she has to cancel her own plans to take care of her mom— later she feels guilty because her mother often reminds her that she can't help being sick. She frequently tells her that she would love to do the things other mothers do, but she was just born frail. Maggie is beginning to find that when she is under a lot of stress, she also gets a headache. Maybe she is just like her mom.

This illustration is not meant to assume that every woman who suffers headaches uses them to consciously or unconsciously be in control. But some of us know we have used illness to get our own way, or at least tried to.

I will admit I am one of those who controlled through sickness. I didn't deal well with stress, so when I had too much to do, I got sick. In that way I controlled the amount of stress that came my way. Instead of having to be the strong, supporting wife or mother, I was the sick one needing to be cared for in bed. My husband and kids would wait on me as I (feebly) protested. It was only through the conviction of the Holy Spirit that I eventually faced up to what I was doing.[3]

The invalid may control through physical or mental symptoms. When a woman is ill, she becomes the focus of the family's life. Every decision made in the family is based on her illness. "How will this affect Mom?" Or, "Will someone be home to take care of Mom?" Or, "Will this make too much noise and bother her?" Or, "I wonder if something I did caused her problem?" Control aims at keeping us at the center of everyone's attention and consideration, and sickness is a powerful way of achieving this end. It is also hard to be angry with an invalid. Children raised with this type of mother are especially vulnerable and tend to grow up with a lot of guilt and a poor self-image: guilt because they deeply resent their mother's inability to care for them, and a poor self-image because they dislike themselves for thinking that way.

As I have already mentioned, indirect control techniques

---

[3] I discuss my healing from this way of controlling in my book *The Delicate Balance of a Woman's Self-Image* (Chosen Books), 1987.

always send a double-message. In the case of the invalid she would say something like, "I wish I were well enough to be a mother to you." And at the same time be thinking, *Being sick is not bad, because it gives me power.* It is easy to see how destructive this double-message can be to relationships. The person who employs sickness to control will also eventually become controlled by the sickness. To give up her sickness would mean giving up her power, and the trade-off would not seem advantageous.

## The Mask

Sylvia was one of the sweetest women that Mark, principal of an elementary school, had ever met. She always apologized for taking his time. "I know you're a very busy man." She was very active in the PTA, and showed a keen interest in her son David's progress. Whenever she called the principal to discuss a problem David was having in class, she made it clear that she wasn't complaining, but she knew Mark was a very kind man and she was sure he would understand. She was so sweet and accommodating that Mark had a hard time mentioning a problem David was having with some of the other boys. Finally, he did tell Sylvia and was astonished at her reaction.

Sylvia exploded and accused him of favoring one of the other boys involved. Mark was so taken by surprise that he could hardly respond to her attack. After that, whenever Mark saw Sylvia around the school she barely acknowledged him.

A woman like Sylvia controls by being overly nice and accommodating. She will show kindness as long as she gets a positive response. In this way she achieves her own ends. However, when she does *not* get her way, the mask falls off. Beneath her sweet exterior is a very angry person. Despite her sweetness, she is very strong-willed and determined to make things happen her way.

This type of hypocritical behavior is used to hide selfishness and self-centeredness, and will also breed hypocrisy in children, who learn by example. They too will learn to play-act and become what others expect them to be—as long as it "works" for their ends! This was the very sin that Jesus warned the Pharisees about when He told them: "On the outside you appear to people as righteous, but on the inside you are full of hypocrisy and wickedness" (Matthew 23:28).

# The Flirt

When Sandy was growing up, she found that she could wrap her father around her finger by acting cute. She would look at her dad with big wide eyes and toss her pretty, blonde curls in a way that rendered her dad powerless to say no to any request she might have had. She had two older brothers, and she also learned how to control them through feminine charms.

Dating became a great game to Sandy. Each prospective date was a challenge to get what she wanted. As soon as her flirtatious behavior "won her man," however, she immediately lost interest and moved on to conquer another unsuspecting male. She loved being a tease and found each new conquest brought a "high," and with it a desire for new challenges.

Now that Sandy is a little older, her playful, teasing way is not quite as attractive. Even Sandy is becoming tired of the constant games she plays and wonders why she is afraid to settle down.

Beneath it all, Sandy has a fear of intimacy. As soon as she succeeds in attracting a man, she fears the exposure of her true self if they develop a close relationship. She projects herself as happy and outgoing, when in reality she is unhappy and frightened. What if one of her conquests really gets to know her? Could he love the *real* Sandy beneath her playful exterior? As long as she controls relationships—keeping men focused on her pretty exterior—she doesn't have to fear exposure. Sadly, she will also forego the joy of a lasting commitment because she keeps everyone at arm's-length.

# The Baby

Debby is only five-feet-two, with the wide, expressive eyes of a child. They are what first attracted her husband Don to her. However, Debby developed the habit of baby-talk to match her childlike appearance, and when her husband confronted her with his wish that she refrain from this kind of talk around their friends, she burst into tears.

Debby is aware of a new problem, but doesn't know what to do about it. Her eyes brim over with tears at the first hint of criticism. She uses tears as an avoidance technique, because she knows that Don and everyone else will immediately back off. Don thought it was appealing at first, but he has begun to feel manipulated by Debby's tears and wonders how he can get her to grow up.

Psychologists are discovering that crying isn't always an emotional release and doesn't always make us feel better. "In fact, sometimes it makes us feel worse. New research findings suggest that crying may be an 'avoidance coping strategy.' People may believe that crying helps them handle their problems, when actually their tears distract them from problem-solving."[4]

We once had a young woman plagued with problems who came to a fellowship meeting in our home. Whenever one of us tried to talk to her about a problem, she would begin to cry. Naturally, we all felt guilty and uncomfortable and quickly changed the subject.

One night her husband told us that he thought she cried to avoid her problems. After gently sharing this with her, she agreed to fight against her desire to cry and inform whoever was talking to her to go right on with what they had to say. In this way, she helped herself to look squarely at an issue. From then on she became closer to all of us, and we were no longer controlled by her tears.

## Sexual Favors

Sadly, sex is a powerful indirect control technique. In the early days of a marriage, the woman often has the control advantage because of the generally stronger sexual drive in a young man. A woman who would loathe being labeled a "sexual object" may subconsciously use her sexual favors as a way of getting what she wants. For example, the night before she asks her husband if they can take that dream vacation, she may "coincidentally" make herself very "available" in her skimpiest nightgown. Contrarily, she may be cold and distant if he tells her that they can't afford a new outfit she had her heart set on.

Many of us learn we can get what we want by catering to a man's strong sexual drive. But the woman who discovers she can control a man through her sexual charms, like Delilah, will eventually emasculate him. The Bible tells us that "the

---

[4]Joan Rachel Goldberg, "Crying It Out," *Health* (February, 1987), pp. 64–66.

wife's body does not belong to her alone but also to her husband" (1 Corinthians 7:4), and a Christian marriage should be based on mutual love and respect for each other's needs and desires—not "power politics."

For men, sexual rejection is total rejection. "When your husband makes a sexual overture to you, he is doing more than asking for sex. He is saying, 'Please accept me.' "[5] If you use his deep need for acceptance to manipulate him, he will probably seek acceptance elsewhere.

## The Belittler

Many women find subtle ways to belittle their husbands as an indirect control tactic. The ultimate goal is to build themselves up while they tear their husband down. Belittling is often done with humor, and the wife will say, "Oh, I was just kidding."

I found myself doing this quite frequently with my husband when we were in the company of other people. I too thought I was "just kidding," but through some careful introspection realized that I joked in public about things which bothered me in private. Rather than sit down and talk to my husband about these issues, I took the cowardly way out and made parodies of them. I also made "cute little jokes" at the dinner table in front of our children. This forced the children to see their father through my eyes. But no child wants to see his father put down, and so the caustic quip usually backfires: The children end up resenting the mother, until she acknowledges her sin and asks their forgiveness. This is exactly what occurred in our case.

A woman may admire a friend's new fur coat with extravagant flattery. The husband is aware that, while the wife is gushing over the coat, she is saying to him, "You are too tight to buy me a gift like this." I know—because I used to do this type of thing. I would make sure my husband knew that "Jack just bought his wife a new sports car, and Sam is taking his wife on a Hawaiian vacation." He knew full well that I was putting him down for not making enough money to do the same for me. To *belittle* does exactly that: It makes the other

---

[5]Barbara De Angelis, *Secrets About Men Every Woman Should Know* (New York: Delacorte Press, 1990), p. 134.

person feel small and insignificant. And because the person then feels like a failure, we use their guilt to keep them under our control.

As I mentioned earlier, there are as many ways of control as there are differing personalities. A woman quickly learns what works with her husband. A newlywed confided that after only three months of marriage, she knew how to get her husband's attention. Instead of nagging him, she would just clam up and answer him in monosyllables. Soon her husband would be following her around the house, begging her to tell him what was wrong. It's amazing how quickly we women can perceive the very thing that will get to our husband.

All these indirect control techniques are an attempt by the woman to control a situation without *appearing* to be in control. The image we portray is very important, so we believe it is safer to go the indirect route. Using manipulative techniques to get control, however, increases anxiety and poor self-image. My prayer is that those of us that are guilty of these attempts at control will come to realize how out-of-control we really are.

The first and most difficult step out of the indirect controller trap is to recognize the problem. We need to take a long, honest look at ourselves and identify the indirect control techniques we may be using with others. Only when we recognize dishonest communication can we relinquish it to God and become truly free.

Although we have touched upon some behaviors we may use to gain our own way, my purpose so far has been to illustrate how direct and indirect control work. Now we will turn our attention in the next three chapters to the emotional roots of control—fear, anger, and shame.

# Section 3

# WHY DO WE CONTROL?

*For God hath not given us the spirit of fear; but of power, and of love, and of a sound mind.*

*2 Timothy 1:7, KJV*

# 6

# *Fear*

Few women set out to control their husbands or dominate their children. Yet society bears testimony to the fact that it is being done. One of the most widespread factors in a woman taking control is *fear*. Even though there may be legitimate reasons for the seeds of fear in us—a sensitive nature, past hurtful experiences, present unfavorable circumstances—what we *do* with fear as adults is our responsibility. We must see fear for what it is—a trap we fall into, causing us to subtly or overtly take wrongful control of the lives of those around us.

## Why Do We Fear?

Fear generally originates from one of three sources.

1. Fear can be an automatic response triggered by the primitive "emotional" brain which controls the involuntary reactions that keep us alive. For example, if you are lying in bed at night and you hear a sudden, dull *thud* from your kitchen, your body will respond by increasing its flow of adrenalin, and greater amounts of blood are instantly shot to your brain and muscles, mobilizing you for fight or flight.

In a situation like this, we cannot voluntarily will ourselves *not* to be afraid. God designed the human body and mind to respond in this way when danger threatens for our own survival.

Some people, however, seem to be especially vulnerable to fear.

2. Fear may be the in-born patterning of our particular nervous system's circuitry. In short, some individuals may be born more sensitive than others, and studies indicate a possible relationship between anxiety and the amount of stress to which an individual was subjected during the period of birth. There also may be health problems that contribute to hypersensitivity, such as a thyroid condition or hypoglycemia.

A person may also become super-sensitized to fear when under an unusual amount of pressure. It has been found that phobias—hyper-fears—are often triggered during a particular time of stress or significant change in life, such as a death in the family, a move out-of-state, or a job change.

Sometimes we experience a sort of low-grade phobia about life itself—a generalized feeling of dread that something terrible is going to happen. A severely sensitized person "may feel [her] heart constantly beating quickly, missing beats, or thumping . . . may have recurring attacks of palpitations . . . may feel [her] stomach churn—especially on waking."[1]

This second type of fear is tormenting, and a person can become crippled by fear. Some women become so subject to this torment they never know when physical symptoms will strike, and their lives become more and more restricted.

3. Fear can become a learned behavior—that is, we learn to fear in certain situations. And as we reach adulthood we can become masters of control in order to keep the discomfort of fear at bay.

A primary "teacher of fear" may be a parent. My mother for instance, was a loving, gentle woman, but she was also very fearful. Her fear was expressed through worry. Her mother, my grandmother, was also a worrier and not without some cause. Deserted by an alcoholic husband, she was left to support herself and her four children. As a single parent, I'm sure she often struggled with anxiety for her family, and outwardly expressed this as worry. Like Grandmother, my mother equated worry with love—"If I love you, I will worry about you." I remember the solemn warnings she would give me when I left the house as a young woman. "Now make sure you

---

[1]Dr. Claire Weekes, *Peace from Nervous Suffering* (New York: Hawthorn Books, Inc., 1972), pp. 2–3.

lock your doors." "Don't drive too fast." "Don't ever drive alone at night." No matter what time I came home, she was waiting up in the living room with a look of painful concern.

When parents are fearful themselves, they communicate fear to their children, especially when the same concerns are voiced over and over. Soon the child feels that the world is a fearful, threatening place.

Worried parents constantly nag their children: "Eat all your vegetables, or you'll get a vitamin deficiency." "Go to bed by ten o'clock, or you'll get sick." "Get out of your wet clothes, or you'll catch a cold." "Don't take a cold drink when you're hot, or it might stop your heart." Transferring fear is one way that some parents control their children's behavior.

If we have been made afraid because of a threat or a perceived danger, we may develop what is commonly known as a phobia—as we mentioned earlier, "an excessive or unreasonable fear that leads a person to avoid a particular object or situation."[2]

It is estimated that "20 to 30 million Americans—the majority of whom are women—have their lives disrupted, their productivity sapped, and their happiness shattered by panic, anxiety and abnormal fear."[3] Most women, it is reported, suffer from one or two phobias: We may be afraid of heights (acrophobic); of being in closed spaces (claustrophobic); of spiders, (arachnophobic); or water (aquaphobic), to name a few. Because these are isolated fears, we feel that if we can avoid the situation we can keep the fear under control.

Whatever the source, fear in any part of our life will limit and keep us from becoming all God wants us to be. And the worst of it is that fear does not remain isolated. Fear has a way of spilling over into other areas of our lives. Eventually, it can become a powerful source of our need to control, for the more fearful we are the more control we need.

## A Painful Journey

I was one of those shy, fearful kind of children. My mother said that I would run and hide when the doorbell rang. After

---

[2]Fredric Neuman, M.D., *Fighting Fear* (New York: Macmillan Publishing Company, Bantam Books, 1985), p. 1.
[3]Mary Peterson Kauffold, "Good News for the Panicked," *Chicago Tribune*, Tempo Woman, Section 6 (Sunday, January 7, 1990), p. 2.

the guests were in the house, I'd creep out, hold on to her leg and peek around at the company. It was considered cute, and I was thought to be just a shy little girl who would eventually outgrow it.

But to me the world seemed full of unknown fear.

I loved my next-door neighbors, the Mitchels—a childless couple in their forties. They "adopted" me and gave me all sorts of extra attention, which coaxed me into their home. One day, however, when I was playing at their house, a doctor came to see Mrs. Mitchel's aged mother, who lived with them. After the doctor left, I was nowhere to be found. A frenzied hunt found me huddled in panic under their bed. To this day I cannot clearly recall what caused the attack of terror that overtook me that day.

The years passed and I did outgrow my shyness. In fact, I gradually swung in the opposite direction because I disliked my mother's worried attitude and vowed I would never be like her. I became socially aggressive in high school and held many offices, eventually getting myself elected vice-president of my class. Finally I felt in control, in charge, on top of everything. I was fearless, and even became somewhat reckless in my college years. I went flying frequently with a boyfriend who owned a Piper Cub airplane. I had my own 22-caliber rifle and often went target shooting. Nothing hinted at the sleeping giant, deep in my emotions, that was about to awaken.

During my fifth year of college, I was living with a roommate in an apartment off campus. One night, I stayed up late studying for finals and also for the Graduate Record Exam. Instead of going into the bedroom and disturbing her sleep, I fell asleep on the couch. Some time later, I awoke from a sound sleep with a feeling of heaviness in my chest.

I sat up in the dark, feeling as if I couldn't breathe. Then I woke up my roommate. She panicked and called an ambulance. By this time I was turning blue around the lips and feeling faint.

When the medical team arrived they administered oxygen and I slowly came around, so that in just a few minutes I was feeling better. Since it didn't appear to be anything serious, the men left me with instructions to see my doctor in the morning. But I didn't sleep the rest of the night. I imagined my lungs collapsing and my heart beating irregularly.

The next day I visited my family doctor who diagnosed my

attack as "nervous collapse." I knew I had been pushing myself, what with studies and tests. I figured that if I submitted to the doctor's prescribed two-week rest and a prescription of tranquilizers, I'd be my old fearless self again.

During those two weeks of recovery I moved home. To my alarm, the panic attacks returned frequently. Often, I'd run into my parent's bedroom in the middle of the night, unable to breathe and very frightened. My mother would reassure me that I was not in any real danger, and eventually I'd fall back into a troubled, restless sleep. I had an increased sense that something big and terrible was stirring inside, and I fought hard to remain in control.

Gradually, the attacks subsided.

The next year I married John Sullivan, a third-year dental school student. One year later, I gave birth to our first child, John. Suddenly, the periods of anxiety reemerged. I would lie in bed at night, my heart pounding, unable to sleep, waiting for John's first cry. Soon I was pregnant again and suffering painful attacks of chest pain, which were later diagnosed as gall bladder problems. After Shannon was born, I had surgery to remove the gall bladder. Over the next several years, I had two more children and two more major operations.

I believe that fear triggered the physical infirmities in me. Many fearful people become subject to physical ailments— some real and some imagined. I had both. If I wasn't really ill, I was thinking about the diseases I might get. If I happened to read a magazine story about a new illness, I immediately felt as if I had the symptoms. It took years before I was delivered from my many illnesses because the real root of my problem was not physical but emotional.

As I neared my thirties, my fears became overwhelming. The panic attacks I'd experienced in college now occurred when I was grocery shopping, or in a department store, or anytime that I had no way to get out of a place or situation. I was forced to sit on an aisle or at the back of an auditorium because it would mean a quick escape. While sitting there, I could picture myself standing up and screaming, or fainting and embarrassing myself. When the feeling would rise to a near panic level, I would quickly get up and leave.

I also developed colitis in fearful situations. I knew the location of every bathroom in the grocery stores, department stores, my children's schools and every other place I might have to be in for more than five minutes. The first thing I did when I went into a new store was to locate the bathroom—in case of an emergency. Naturally, my life became more and more restricted, and I became better and better at making up excuses.

Today I know that I was suffering from agoraphobia, "a marked fear of being alone or of being in public places from which escape might be difficult or help not available in case of sudden incapacitation."[4] Twenty years ago, I thought I had the attacks because I was losing my mind. This particular phobia, which experts say is rampant among women today, means that fear has taken total control. It is not fear of a given place, situation or crowd, but rather a fear of the *feelings* that the place, situation or crowd stirs up in us. We are afraid that we will get hysterical, have a heart attack, or be unable to breath. Generally, it is the fear of being out of control of ourselves or our environment.

## The Spread of Fear

If you are a fearful person, you may already be aware of how your fear spreads and causes other serious problems. The Empress Alexandra's fear for her son eventually became a health issue and . . . "she began to develop a whole series of symptoms which she referred to as the result of 'an enlarged heart.' She had shortness of breath, and exertion became an effort. . . . In modern medical terminology, the Empress Alexandra undoubtedly was suffering from psychosomatic anxiety symptoms brought on by worry over the health of her son."[5] She very seldom traveled or left the palace. Her world was her family. Her fears may well have been planted when her mother died suddenly. This traumatic event dramatically altered her personality from happy and outgoing to withdrawn and somber. A tragic event is often a violent reminder of our mortality and the lack of control we really have over our life. As a result, it may trigger a desire to always be in control, as if that will keep the unexpected from occurring.

The woman who must have control is a fearful woman. She

---

4Neuman, p. 4.
5Robert K. Massie, *Nicholas and Alexandra* (New York: Dell Publishing Co., Inc., 1967), p. 161.

needs to have increased control over her life, while her world becomes smaller and smaller.

Not only does fear spread itself into a woman's physical body, it also spreads into her *relationships*.

## Fear of Relationships

The June 9, 1989, *Oprah Winfrey Show* was on the topic, "Daughters of Divorce." Though this program fell far short of a documentary, it did touch upon the leading fear of women today—a fear of relationships, and specifically of becoming dependent upon a man.

Because of the record-high divorce rate in our country, many women have been raised without fathers. In addition, some mothers teach their children, either consciously or unconsciously, never to trust a man. Our generation of women has been raised to be financially independent so that they will not have to depend on their husband's income in case the marriage breaks up. Some of us enter marriage with an "escape-clause" mentality, and do not fully commit to the relationship because we're afraid our husband will do to us what our father did to our mother.

One mother on the program told about taking her daughters to see their father's car parked out in front of his girlfriend's house when he was supposed to be bowling. One of the daughters, now thirty-five and single, lamented, "I want to be married but I have a hard time trusting men because of my father's infidelity. I'm afraid of being trapped."

Another women commented, "When we women pulled together and made men the enemy, that gave us power. But now we find our relationships don't work."

Kay is a woman who found that her marriage relationship was not working. Even though Kay and her husband were both committed Christians, Kay lived in fear that her marriage would fall apart or that her husband Frank would cheat on her. Kay's father had left her mother after eighteen years of marriage, and as a teenager Kay heard the arguments over his infidelities. Then she saw her mother completely fall apart after the divorce.

"Mom made the marriage her whole life, and when it fell apart so did she," Kay says. "I determined that would *never* happen to me. I would be the one in control."

Kay quickly learned how—with subtle looks of disapproval or with stolid noncommittal to Frank's ideas or wishes—to control almost every aspect of their relationship. This included how money was spent, where they went, whom they spent time with and even their intimate life. Frank kept trying to "read" Kay's signals, but very quickly became frustrated. If he had not been a sincere Christian, he might have walked out on her long before this. In fact, he had no real interest in any other woman. He truly loved Kay.

"And all along," Kay admitted, "I kept up a wall between Frank and me. I guarded my emotions. That way, if Frank left me I wouldn't have totally 'lost it' like my mother."

For the first two years of her marriage, Kay did not realize the tremendous tension involved in keeping her emotions to herself, or that her failure to commit totally to Frank was insuring the failure of her marriage. She believed that if she controlled her level of commitment, she would be in control of the marriage.

In their third year of marriage, she came for counseling about a serious problem. Like Job, what she had feared was about to come upon her. Frank finally was attracted to another woman in the church, and Kay often saw them talking together. To her, this spelled the beginning of the end of their marriage.

Through counseling, Kay came to understand how fear had actually caused a self-fulfilling prophecy to take place in her life. She saw that she had to face directly her fear of abandonment, instead of trying to control Frank by withholding her emotional commitment to him. She also realized that even if the very worst happened she and God together could face it.

The first step Kay had to take was to forgive her father for leaving the family. Then she prayed, asking God to help her release Frank from the judgment she had transferred from her father onto him: "Men are selfish creatures who abandon their wives and children"; "Frank is probably no better than any other man—even though he is a Christian."

In a later session, she asked God to walk closely beside her the moment old fears rose up, causing her to protectively withdraw. She committed herself to handing over those fears to Him and asking for His peace to come upon her. The responsibility of the marriage was now in God's hands, rather than in hers.

When we met again some time later, Kay shared the continuing freedom and understanding that were beginning to take the place of fear and mistrust. She had finally realized that at the base of it all she had been placing her trust in the wrong person.

"I know now that if we put all our trust in people, they will come short of our expectations," Kay shared. "When I was in control, I put both Frank and myself under tremendous pressure to make the marriage work. The harder we tried, the worse our relationship became. My constant suspicion and lack of trust eventually could have driven Frank into the very thing I feared—the arms of another woman. Now I am beginning to relax, because I am committed to keeping my trust in God."

In the Gospel of John there is an intriguing statement: "Jesus didn't trust them, for he knew mankind to the core. No one needed to tell him how changeable human nature is!" (John 2:24, 25, TLB). At first glance, this seems to indicate that Jesus was an aloof, suspicious person. But we know that is far from the truth. Jesus remained totally committed and vulnerable in His relationships—even with Judas. But because He fully understood the frailty of human nature, He knew it was senseless to base His faith or His emotional responses upon the actions of another human being. Instead, He trusted God first. Kay learned that it was actually *unfair* to put her complete trust in Frank rather than in God, thus forcing Frank to give her assurances only God can give. She learned that she could trust the grace of God in Frank. Because of this, their marriage today, ten years later, is healthy and strong.

Today's widespread fear of trusting men can actually become the catalyst that causes us to place our trust and faith in God. The stress that comes when we attempt to be in control of relationships will ultimately rob us of the joy of life. We can become free of that stress when we release our control to God, and begin to live in freedom from fear.

I must say it here for emphasis: The first step out of fear is to give total control to Jesus Christ. That was my first step on a ten-year journey. If you have never made Jesus Lord of your life, I invite you to open your heart to Him now in prayer. Ask Him to become alive in you by the power of His Holy Spirit. (Read John 3.)

If you are a Christian woman who is recognizing for the

first time that the windows of your soul are clouded with fear, so that you look upon your life with distrust and dread, I invite you also, through prayer, to allow our Lord to come into the cold, distrustful inner room of your soul and warm it with the fire of His peace. Maybe you have been looking for a long time for that promised "peace of God that passes all understanding" (Philippians 4:7). Today, it can radiantly transform you as you allow the stubble of mistrust to be consumed in the fire of His great love for you, through which no eternal harm can ever come. (See Romans 8.)

*In your anger do not sin . . . and do not give
the devil a foothold.*

*Ephesians 4:26, 27*

# 7

# *Anger*

Patti had spent hours in the kitchen preparing a wonderful oriental dinner, complete with Chinese tea and fortune cookies. Her husband and three children were now seated around the table, chopsticks in hand, waiting to begin. She placed the large wok in the center of the table. As her ten-year-old daughter Julie reached for the serving spoon, she spilled her milk.

"You clumsy oaf!" Patti's shrill remark startled the whole family. She threw a dish towel at Julie and yelled, "Wipe it up, before it gets all over the floor."

Julie sat paralyzed by the cutting words.

"I *said*, wipe it up! Are you deaf?" Patti repeated impatiently.

Julie began to cry. Patti's husband Tim said quietly, "She didn't do it on purpose, Patti. I'll help her clean up."

His even tone infuriated Patti. "You always take *their* side," she accused. "I suppose it's my fault she spilled her milk! Why is it that I work so hard to make things *nice* around here, while the rest of you just relax and take advantage of my hard work?"

Tim knew better than to try to reason with Patti during one of her "episodes." Instead, he wiped up the spilled milk and poured another glass for Julie.

By this time Patti had settled down and was feeling foolish and guilty about her outburst. The three children sat completely still. "Well, let's eat before the food gets cold," she said in a subdued voice.

The children very carefully helped themselves to the food. Everyone made a point to compliment Patti on the dinner. There was a cautious air about their mealtime, however, and the special-dinner atmosphere had vanished. Afterward, all the kids went to work like dutiful, silent soldiers, clearing the table, washing the dishes, quietly retreating to their rooms to do their homework before being asked.

Patti noticed the tension on the children's faces all evening, and felt increasingly bad about her angry outburst. Why did this periodically happen? Usually she was a tolerant, caring mother. Maybe she should start watching her calendar. She'd read about PMS (pre-menstrual syndrome) in a women's magazine and wondered if her sudden anger might be connected to the cyclical rise and fall of hormones.

On the other hand, Patti is aware that her children and husband respond in a seemingly positive manner to her anger. Tim becomes especially attentive and the children do everything she asks without having to be told ten times. It's as if they don't notice or appreciate all her hard work until she loses her temper. Then they are grateful—for a few days, anyway.

But there is another worrisome factor.

Her stomach has been bothering her lately, and Patti wonders if she's developing an ulcer. Deep down she senses that anger is controlling too much of her life and she's been having a difficult time doing anything about it. Maybe she should see the counselor at church.

## Where Anger Finds a Foothold

A strong emotion will often make an impression on someone else's spirit and force them to respond. Since anger is the strongest emotion, we often resort to it to make the strongest impression.

Anger, in short, is the quickest means of making a point— the quickest way to say, "Pay attention to me!" without saying the words. Many women know that an angry outburst is the surest way to get their husband to "snap to attention."

There are three major reasons why a woman's anger gains a foothold in the life of a man.

1. Many men do not know how to manage their own feelings toward a woman—especially hostile feelings. Most men

have a deep-seated aversion to fighting with a woman, both because they're afraid of their greater physical strength, and in many cases a woman has the upper hand when it comes to a verbal fight. Though women have been traditionally discouraged from showing physical aggression, "the norms of proper behavior do allow women to express their feelings in words—and the angry barb, the rapier-sharp putdown long have been considered women's special province."[1] The increase of wife-abuse in this country indicates that more and more men are turning to physical abuse. Most men, however, will simply withdraw.

Gordon Dalbey, author of *Healing the Masculine Soul*, says that many men grow up with angry, demanding mothers and passive fathers. "Often, the man who grew up with such parents has seen his mother's anger flare up and ultimately become destructive without a strong father to counter it with manly restraint. He has thus learned to fear the woman's anger, and is anxious to suppress his wife's rage even when it is not directed at him."[2]

Jack is a successful businessman, a tough-minded competitor and a dynamo at work. However, when he comes through the front door of his home, his decisive attitude retreats and he becomes passive. His wife Cindy is constantly on edge. Her anger simmers beneath the surface like a steaming teakettle. Jack doesn't know how to deal with it. At work he can confront an angry employee, get the issues out on the table, and forcefully tell him to "shape up." But he can't use that tactic with Cindy. She loves to argue and debate, and if he does score a point in an argument, she dissolves in tears and says something like, "I can't believe you would say something that would hurt me so much. You have no idea how much you hurt me." And so, his power undercut, he comes out the loser—again. He knows the safest ploy at home is to remain invisible—to simply "tune out."

2. The foothold a woman's anger gains is illustrated by Cindy's tears: Most men feel terrible if they make a woman cry or get upset. One of a man's strongest drives toward a woman is that of protector: To cause a woman emotional pain

---

[1]Shari Miller Sims, "Getting Physical," *Chicago Tribune*, Tempo Woman, (June 11, 1989), pp. 1, 7.
[2]Gordon Dalbey, *Healing the Masculine Soul* (Waco, Tex.: Word Books, 1988), p. 66.

goes against this protective drive. In the face of a woman's tears, he can become distracted and may even overlook the original problem. He becomes focused on the "obvious": He has been a "brute" once again.

Nita was stopped by a policeman for running a stop sign. Her two children in the back seat stared with wide, frightened eyes at the intimidating man in the dark blue uniform. While Nita told the policeman that her husband would be furious about the ticket, a tear trickled down her cheek. The officer, afraid she would burst into tears at any moment, mumbled something about being more careful from now on, and that he wouldn't give her a ticket this time.

In his book *Healing the Shame That Binds You*, John Bradshaw says many girls from an early age learn to convert anger into sadness. In fact, as he puts it, "Crying when feeling angry is a common female racket."[3]

3. Men are afraid that if they get a woman upset or angry enough she may leave them. Dalbey says this "reflects the boy's fear of the mother who, when she sees her son growing up and away from her, may threaten to withdraw affection from him by pouting or manipulating against his growing strength in an effort to hold on to him. . . . He is apparently forced to choose between his manhood and the woman's love—and without a father to stand with him in manly truth, he can only abdicate his strength to the woman."[4]

Rob and his mother have a great relationship most of the time. Since he started high school, though, she seems jealous of his involvement in sports. She loves to brag to her friends about his position as quarterback, but she seems cold and distant whenever he tells her he won't be home for dinner because of practice. She makes him feel guilty for being gone so much, and he will occasionally cancel his evening plans to be home with her.

As women, we may find we are actually rewarded for our emotional outbursts—or, we may not be conscious of the fact that we dominate with our anger. Either way, the results are the same. Things go along the way we want them to—close to it, anyway—or the simmering emotions inside will boil over.

---

[3]John Bradshaw, *Healing the Shame that Binds You* (Deerfield Beach, Fla.: Health Communications, Inc., 1988), p. 77.
[4]Dalbey, p. 74.

I am not saying that you and I will ever escape the *impulse* of anger when confronted by something bothersome, or that we should simply squelch it so that we appear to be "good Christians." Squelched anger is damaging. In fact, squelching it as a lifelong habit is probably one of the reasons we use it to control: It has controlled us.

Nonetheless, using our anger on others to manipulate them into doing what we want is sin. The rewards of anger are short-lived. Controlling by emotional outbursts may give us a foothold in someone else's life, but constant anger can have a malignant foothold in our own soul that eats away like a spiritual cancer.

## The Three Prongs of Anger

If we use anger as a tool to control, soon it will have control over us. In fact, Scripture warns that it will become like a devil's trident, with a three-pronged grip on us, emotionally, physically, and spiritually. We need to see the effects of this evil tool in all three areas, and recognize how it has gained power over us.

### Emotional Effects

Parents often assume that anger is basically a masculine emotion. Because of this, they discourage anger in their daughters. Since anger is "unfeminine" and "unacceptable," girls often convert it into a more tolerable feeling such as guilt, hurt or sadness. But ignored anger will eventually cause more serious problems.

Dr. Milton Layden, in his perceptive book *Escaping the Hostility Trap*, says that depression results in those children who were punished when they spoke up or showed anger. In this way they were conditioned to keep their angry feelings inside. "Habitual suppression of [hostility] may also arise from other forms of emotional conditioning—as when, after ten years of arguments with her husband, a woman decides that harmony can be achieved only by giving in and keeping her feelings to herself."[5]

Buried anger, which turns to depression, is a powerful way

---

[5]Milton Layden, *Escaping the Hostility Trap* (Englewood Cliffs, N.J.: Prentice-Hall, Inc., 1977), p. 196.

of controlling one's environment. Everyone in the household is controlled by the depressed mood of one person. A depressed wife silently punishes her husband and children. What right do they have to be happy when she is suffering? Paul J. Gelinas, a psychologist and educator, says, "In many years as a clinical psychologist working with young adults, I cannot recall a single case of neurosis or emotional disturbance that did not have unresolved anger as the main overt or intrinsic element in the disorder."[6]

Margo's mother often told her it was *shameful* to be angry, so Margo learned to repress her anger, hold it inside and ignore it. Eventually her unresolved anger turned into depression, and only after Margo began seeing a counselor did she realize a layer of frustration had settled, like a dull film of dust, over the years of "unacceptable" anger she had suppressed.

Everyone else in the house may be dominated by anger-turned-depression in one family member, but soon the depression dominates the person who has repressed anger. Chemical changes in the depressed person's brain will actually continue the depression. A popular theory concludes that depression occurs because of some malfunction of chemicals in the brain that makes certain individuals susceptible. However, Dr. Layden says, "It is likelier that chemical changes in the depressive's brain are produced by stress and strain, and not the other way around, since anyone conditioned to suppress [hostility] reacts with depression to disrespect."[7]

Anger-turned-depression can have a second effect on our emotions. It affects the *emotional communication* we give off to others. They may pick up our emotional signals and internalize them. Naturally, this would most affect those who are the closest to us, and our rejection and isolation can be transmitted to them by means of looks, words and body language.

John and I discovered how strongly this may be at work in a relationship in our counseling with the couple who run our rehabilitation center, Manny and Jean. Married for five years, both are former drug-abusers who have been strong, committed Christians for seven years. So we were surprised when they brought up a serious problem they were having in their marriage. Manny said he couldn't deal with Jean's anger

[6]Paul J. Gelinas, *Coping With Anger* (New York: The Rosen Publishing Group, Inc., 1979), p. 15.
[7]Layden, p. 195.

any more. During the day he could escape her angry looks and impatient tone of voice by leaving the apartment. But at night, as soon as he walked in, he could feel her disapproval and anger.

"If I roll over in bed and disturb her, I hear her sigh and make little annoyed sounds. So I try to lie very still. I'm afraid I'll snore and she'll get angry. I can't even relax in my own bed," said Manny, "so now I sleep on the couch."

Manny wasn't the only one who felt rejected and isolated. Jean also felt rejected by Manny's exodus to the living room at night, and this only increased her anger. She didn't feel she was sending angry signals to Manny, and in her mind the problem was all his. If he would only show her love and acceptance, she believed any anger she might have would disappear. Yet she agreed to meet for prayer about the situation.

Several nights later in our meeting with Jean, our discussion revealed that her mother had controlled her with repressed anger.

"She was never outwardly angry, but her looks and impatient tone of voice told me I didn't please her," Jean said. "My mother was a perfectionist, and I always felt I couldn't measure up."

"Your mother controlled you with anger—has it become an effective way to control Manny?" I posed. The surprised look on Jean's face told me she had never seen the similarity.

"Are you telling me I'm like my mother?" Jean asked in a disbelieving voice.

I knew that Jean would not easily see the similarity, so I went on to explain that when we place judgment on a person, we can become like the person we judge. It is a simple, psychological maxim: Whatever dominates your conscious thought will control your emotions and your actions. Because we focus on the negative actions of the one we judge, their image becomes our image. I also explained that Proverbs 20:20 gives some understanding as to why we often can't see how much we become like our parents when we judge them harshly: "God puts out the light of the man who curses his father or mother" (TLB). When we judge our parents, our understanding becomes darkened, and we repeat their failures and excesses.

We prayed with Jean for release from her judgment on her mother and for courage to forgive her for her perfectionistic control. We also asked Jean to forgive herself for her past failures and for falling short of her own standards.

Jean saw for the first time that she was giving her husband the same conditional love her mother had given her. Once she was able to see how she manipulated him through repressed anger, she began learning to deal with it and establish new, positive habits of response.

## Physical Effects

The second prong of anger wounds the physical body. Over the long haul, anger will affect your health. Medical periodicals such as *The New England Journal of Medicine* have published studies indicating that mismanaged anger is perhaps the principal factor involved in predicting cardiovascular disease. Dr. Layden says that suppressed hostility is the main cause of insomnia, fatigue, headaches, ulcers, high blood pressure and heart attacks. He states: "Ninety percent of a group of migraine patients I treated at Johns Hopkins Hospital were relieved of their excruciating headaches by learning to rid themselves of [hostility]."[8] Anger stimulates the release of the same hormones that are produced under stress and fear. They affect the heart rhythm, elevate blood pressure, raise the blood-sugar level, constrict the blood vessels in the digestive tract, and produce feelings of excitement and anxiety. It is easy to see why a lifetime of repressed anger can wreak havoc on the body.

My friend Donna learned the hard way how repressed anger could affect her health. Her husband, Joe, opened a tropical fish import business that went bankrupt within a year. After that, Joe went through several months of unemployment and part-time low-paying jobs. During this time Donna began to experience a ringing in her ears, dizziness and spells of vomiting, which were eventually diagnosed as Meniere's Disease.

Donna came for prayer and spiritual counsel and discovered that she had never really forgiven Joe, his business partner, or God for the financial failure. On the surface she had accepted what had happened, but deep down felt she had a right to be angry. After she forgave each of them, she went without an episode of ear trouble for eight months.

---

[8]Layden, p. 159.

Then Donna had a confrontation with a relative, and found herself seething with anger. That same night she was awakened from sleep by the dizziness and nausea. She realized that she had allowed anger and unforgiveness to seep back into her life and had violated the scriptural principle, "Do not let the sun go down while you are still angry, and do not give the devil a foothold" (Ephesians 4:26–27). When she realized what she had done, she immediately prayed and forgave her relative for the offense and, in doing so, eliminated the devilish prong. Donna now believes that she will remain free from Meniere's Disease as she walks in daily forgiveness.

Anger is a powerful emotion—the most powerful. Imagine the destructive force of mismanaged anger on our internal organs. While we cannot attribute all our physical ills to suppressed anger, there is general agreement among medical doctors that many illnesses do stem from a root of anger.

## Spiritual Effects

The third prong of anger is seen in the spiritual response. We will look at this in light of the three roots of anger—frustration, inferiority and past anger.

*Frustration.* Clinical psychologist Paul Gelinas says, "Many other researchers in the field of human conduct have concluded that 'aggression is always the consequence of frustration.' More simply stated, whenever we feel blocked in getting what we really desire and need for our well-being, our survival, we tend to become angry and are inclined to fight for our right to exist. . . . The frustration-aggression hypothesis simply states that if our needs are not met, we become frustrated and then angry."[9]

Each of us has a different level of frustration-tolerance, depending on how well we've learned to cope when things don't go our way. Because I was raised by a perfectionistic father who erupted angrily at every little frustration, I too had a very low frustration level. I once kicked a washing machine that refused to spin dry and broke my toe. I have yelled, "*Stupid* thing!" at a peanut butter jar I couldn't open. And I have been known to throw a child's "new math" book across the room because I couldn't understand it. For some of us, our days are filled with these types of petty frustrations that last

---

[9]Gelinas, pp. 10, 11.

a few seconds and are quickly forgotten. But what about those frustrations that are more serious—frustrations that last for years? What about the single mom who doesn't receive the promised child-support and lacks the skills to obtain a well-paying job? Or the intelligent black woman who is passed over for promotion because of racial prejudice? Or the single woman who has to forego any social life because she cares for her invalid mother? The Bible says, "Hope deferred makes the heart sick" (Proverbs 13:12), and constant frustration will certainly affect our spiritual life.

When Marie came to see me, she was concerned about her backslidden condition. At one time, she'd been an ardent Christian, heavily involved in ministry in her local church. She told me she had not attended church for a year and a half, and what really frightened her was that she didn't miss it a bit.

Marie's husband was an alcoholic and a verbally abusive man. She lived with constant criticism and attacks on her self-esteem. At one time, Marie had had a strong hope that her husband would become a Christian and their marriage would be restored. Now, fifteen years later, she'd lost all hope for any change in their relationship. Even more frustrating, not one of her three children had any relationship with God.

Marie was a totally frustrated woman. Her frustration had turned into anger toward God who, she felt, had failed her. When I pointed this out to Marie, she acknowledged that she had indeed presented God with her list of expectations and was angry that He had not answered her.

As Marie and I counseled together, she discovered that her frustration stemmed from an attitude that caused her to believe everything should go according to her plans. This attitude was in direct conflict with her understanding that when she gave her life to Christ, she had pledged to submit to His plan for her life. She had failed to release the small daily frustrations to God as well as the major ones. Most of her frustration came because she didn't really believe God was concerned about her situation or that He really heard her prayers.

I suggested that Marie begin to look up scripture verses that stress the goodness of God to us, His children. I too had had to change my false ideas of a punitive and judgmental God, so I could learn to trust. From my own struggles, I was able to assure Marie that God did want the same things she wanted—the salvation of her husband and children—but she had to release the *how* and *when* to Him.

Marie was also struggling with the guilt that she was somehow to blame: If she had been doing the right thing, after all, she would see results. I reminded her that we are to plant the seed and water it, but it is God who gives the growth (1 Corinthians 3:6). Marie and I prayed together and she confessed her frustration and anger. Then she recommitted herself to God and her home situation to His keeping. Marie has had to reinforce her commitment with a daily prayer of trust in God, but she is once again excited about Christianity and God's plan for her life, expectant of His answer and yet at rest in a new level of faith.

*Inferiority*. Frustration is one of the roots of anger; Dr. Layden reveals another: "When we do not feel respected by others, our opinion of our own worth is lowered . . . we experience lack of respect as a relative feeling of inferiority . . . The degree of hostility produced is determined by the degree of inferiority we feel at any given time. Note how kind, sympathetic, and unselfish you're apt to become after a successful accomplishment and how irritable-prone you are after a failure."[10]

If your husband makes a "parting-shot" remark in the morning like, "It'd be nice if you could get this messy house cleaned up," you'll probably explode with inappropriate anger when little Jimmy drops clay all over the rug. On the other hand, if on departure you get a kiss and a compliment, Jimmy's spill will most likely meet with a magnanimous, "Don't worry, Mommy will help you get that cleaned up."

Whether it's a put-down from our husband, criticism from our boss or Christian leader, or a hurtful remark from our child, when we feel bad about ourselves, we don't handle stress well. Dr. Layden's solution is not to try to elevate our low self-esteem but to try to understand the other person: "Whenever anyone belittles, acts superior, or is hostile to you, think of who or what's been bugging *him*."[11] Scripture says the same thing: "Do nothing out of selfish ambition or vain conceit, but in humility consider others better than yourselves. Each of you should look not only to your own interests, but also to the interests of others" (Philippians 2:3–4). As we follow this bib-

---

[10]Layden, pp. 9, 10.
[11]Layden, p. 33.

lical admonition we find that our hostile feelings disappear. When we bestow honor and respect on others, we find that God bestows honor and respect on us.

Place yourself in this situation: You are a nurse, working in an under-staffed hospital on the surgical floor. A new supervisor takes over who is rude, and accuses you of being inefficient. You would probably feel very angry with her. But what if another nurse tells you that your supervisor's youngest child just committed suicide? Your outlook would change immediately, and you would be able to tolerate her rudeness, because you would see through it to her underlying pain.

None of us really knows the pain in another's heart, and when we respond in tolerance and understanding to rudeness we find that our feeling of anger, arising from inferiority, begins to fade away.

*Past unforgiveness.* Current frustration and feelings of inferiority may lead to some anger, but I believe most anger is rooted in the past.

Jan found this to be true—and with her understanding she received an unexpected bonus. Jan and her husband were in our Sunday night home-fellowship meeting, and one evening she asked us to pray with her about her anger.

"I wake up angry, and don't know why," Jan confessed.

We asked several questions seeking to learn the source of her anger, but everything at home seemed to be fine. We all agreed to pray and fast for her on Wednesday of the following week. Our prayer would be that God would reveal to her the source of her anger.

At that time Jan was having a problem with TMJ (temporal mandibular joint disfunction—severe facial pain caused by misalignment of the jaw), and was unable to eat because of the pain. She decided to begin her fast on Tuesday since she could not eat anyway.

Jan had been raised by a perfectionistic, authoritarian father who constantly found fault with her. One of her deepest hurts was that he had not allowed her to have braces as a child. This caused deep wounds and tears throughout her teenage years, and Jan decided that when she was old enough to pay for them herself, she would have braces. Finally, after she and her husband had paid for braces for all three of their children, it was Jan's turn. She went to an orthodontist for the X-rays and impressions in preparation. But the orthodontist found that she had waited too long. He explained to her that the work should have been done when she was twelve. Several of her lower teeth were pushed so far out of alignment that to correct her bite now would require breaking her jaw in three places, removing several teeth, and wiring her jaw shut for six to eight weeks—with no guarantee that it would relieve the TMJ symptoms.

As Jan fasted and prayed, all these previous events surfaced, and she realized the tremendous anger she held against her father for refusing to let her have braces as a child. She didn't want to forgive him and give up her pain. She wanted to let him know how much he had hurt her. Even though she'd never confronted him with her anger, she'd often imagined scenes in which she lashed out at him. Recently she'd relished the idea of one day telling him that her TMJ problem was his fault because he hadn't allowed her to have braces. She wanted to hurt him the way he'd hurt her. On Wednesday, as we all fasted and prayed, she was able to forgive her father and release him from the judgment she held against him.

Jan's is one of those stories that has a remarkable too-good-to-be-true ending. She was immediately healed of TMJ because, in her case, its cause was triggered by a deep root of bitterness and anger. Better still, she was healed of years of anger and unforgiveness that were poisoning her life. Jan's problem was very deep-rooted, and she believes that if she hadn't been fasting and praying she might not have discovered its cause and been healed.

Past pain and unforgiveness are often the reason for our present anger. Anger gets piled on top of anger until it only takes a small offense to set the pile tumbling down and spilling over all those who are unfortunate enough to be in its path. Like Jan, we need to let the Holy Spirit reveal to us past situations that have caused us anger, clearly face them, and then release them to God.

Often, a good tip-off that something from the past is eating away at us is a reaction which is way out of proportion to the problem. When your husband makes a remark about your hair and you throw the hairspray at him, it's time to look for a deeper root.

Instead of concentrating on the things that irritate you today, ask God to show you where the anger is rooted. Setting aside a day for prayer and fasting is a good way to loosen the hold anger may have on various areas of your life. Once you see the root, pray for God's forgiveness—for yourself and then toward the others who were involved in your past. This is the surest way to destroy the foothold anger has on your spirit.

There is another major way in which hurt and buried anger infuse a person's soul. It is so major that it requires an entire chapter to deal with it. I'm referring to the buried hurt and anger that turns into *shame*.

Many of us do not identify with the word shame at first glance. You may say, "I don't feel any shame. Shame is what you feel if you're an addict or a criminal or a prostitute." Before you conclude that, however, allow me to help you look at some of the deeper meanings of shame and at some of its roots. Then you can determine whether or not it has affected your life.

*The man and his wife were both naked, and
they felt no shame.*

*Genesis 2:25*

# 8

# *Shame*

Sandy stepped off the school bus in front of her home and felt her stomach tighten instinctively with the familiar rush of anxiety. What would her mom be like today? Sandy never knew.

Some days she'd find her mother in the kitchen, humming along with the radio, smiling while making supper. Sandy would let out a deep breath and relax. On other days, she'd walk into an ominously quiet house. She would head straight for her mom's bedroom to find her sprawled across the bed in a drunken stupor. She would then cover her mother with a blanket and begin to straighten up the house, throwing away the liquor bottles before her dad got home from work. She would cook something simple such as beans and franks for dinner, and wait for her younger brother to get home from school. She would try to keep him quiet and make him do his homework in the kitchen with her.

The biggest problem was during school vacations. Sandy never invited her friends over, because she was afraid her mom might start drinking. Sandy usually stayed inside and read— one reason she was a straight-A student. She wished she had someone to talk to, but Sandy felt she had to keep her mom's drinking a secret. Her dad always reminded her of how much he depended on his "good girl" to keep things stable at home— and to keep their "problem" under wraps.

There are too many "Sandys" among us—women who

grew up in environments where they were abused emotionally or physically, and left to bear the responsibilities of someone else's unhealthy or destructive behavior.

A woman who grows up in this kind of environment develops a vague uneasiness, like a shadow that haunts her. She has learned to keep a secret, to bury her own needs and feelings, to pretend. The problem is, she often is uneasy, wondering what other people think or feel about her. That is because she hardly knows what to think about herself. Her own natural judgment has been overridden so many times by those who "know better." She often feels unprepared for life and struggles hard to be consistent, especially in her emotions. She is her own worst critic, but protects herself by struggling to maintain rigid controls in her life so others will not find fault with her.

Does any of this sound familiar? You are not alone.

I've met many women like Sandy in twenty years of teaching and counseling—women who are haunted by a shadow. I've learned that the shadow has a name—*shame*. Shame "refers to humiliation so painful, embarrassment so deep, and a sense of being so completely diminished that one feels he or she will disappear into a pile of ashes."[1]

Shame affects your entire *self*, convinces you that you are not good enough, deficient, God's colossal mistake. A person who feels shamed, like Sandy, will have a desire to control. This is motivated not by a drive for power but rather a drive for *predictability, safety*, and most of all, *respect*. Since she had no control over the shameful experiences of her early life, she desires to make sure her life will be free from spontaneity and surprise, which might bring shameful exposure. She would extend this control to others in her environment—her husband, children, friends. The one who really suffers, though, is the shamed woman herself.

Because inwardly she chastises, rebukes, belittles or drives herself unmercifully, she lives *defensively*. Spontaneous and authentic responses are difficult in relationships. In her search for predictability and security she is willing to trade away the chance for real and meaningful relationships.

---

[1]Merle A. Fossum & Marilyn J. Mason, *Facing Shame* (New York: W. W. Norton & Company, 1986), p. xii.

# The Core Emotion

When Adam and Eve were first placed in that perfect garden, they were without shame, without self-consciousness. As soon as they violated the command of God, they experienced guilt, then felt shame. They realized they were naked and sewed fig leaves together to cover themselves (Genesis 3:7). We see that guilt is a sense that comes when we violate the law. Shame, in contrast, is the sense that we are not good enough and that we must "cover" ourselves so that no one else will detect the "truth" about us and dismiss us.

Today, many psychologists believe that shame may be the core emotion from which all other negative ones receive their energy. Shame is one of the first emotions that Adam and Eve experienced, and their reaction to it is identical to human behavior today. The first effect is a "feeling of being exposed, of having your inner-self revealed to the world and shown to be flawed, unworthy, irredeemably bad."[2] Adam and Eve's sensation of nakedness had more to do with the exposure of their sinful nature than with their lack of clothing. Throughout the Bible, nakedness and sinfulness are parallel thoughts. In the book of Revelation, for example, Jesus exhorts the Laodicean church to buy from Him "white clothes to wear, so you can cover your shameful nakedness" (Revelation 3:18).

Second, there is "the impulse to cover up and divert attention from the inner self, which has been exposed."[3] Adam and Eve made leaf aprons to cover their nakedness; many of us escape by creating a "false self." One definition of false is "not genuine; counterfeit; fake." We learn to hide the real person inside—believing it to be weak, silly, worthy of despising—and to cover it with shows of strength or goodness or rightness.

From this internalized judgment against ourselves springs many false faces—none of them representing our true selves. "The false self is always more or less than human. The false self may be a perfectionist or a slob, family hero or a family scapegoat. As the false self is formed, the authentic self may go into hiding. Years later the layers of defense and pretense are so intense that one loses all awareness of who one really is."[4]

---

[2] Mary Ellen Donovan, "SHAME, the Secret Emotion," *Ladies Home Journal* (May, 1989), pp. 70, 72–74.
[3] Ibid.
[4] John Bradshaw, *Healing the Shame That Binds You* (Deerfield Beach, Fla.: Health Communications, Inc., 1988), p. 14.

The most crippling characteristic of shame is that it is a *secret* emotion. We may be free to express other emotions like joy, anger, sadness, or, if not to express them, at least to admit to having them. But we hide shame from others—and often from ourselves. When we attempt to hide our shame, however, we again fall into the control trap.

## Guilt Versus Shame

Not one of us has managed to make it through life without suffering guilt from infractions of God's moral law—we tell our mother our room is cleaned up, and she goes to look; we get caught taking typing paper or other supplies home from our workplace; our husband finds the new dress we hid in the closet so he wouldn't know we were out shopping again; our children overhear us telling a "white lie" to a neighbor. In these situations we may experience the blush that accompanies the feeling of guilt.

John Bradshaw says in his insightful book *Healing the Shame That Binds You*: "Blushing is the manifestation of our human limits . . . With blushing we know we've made a mistake. Why would we have such a capacity, if mistakes were not part of our essential nature?"[5]

Guilt is a healthy human emotion. It warns us that we have violated God's moral law. It is the still, small voice of God reminding us that we are ultimately responsible to Him for our behavior. God has provided a remedy for guilt—we are to confess our guilt to Him (1 John 1:9), and to our brothers and sisters in the family of God (James 5:16). Our confession brings God's forgiveness and restoration to fellowship.

Shame, on the other hand, is a destructive force. "*To have shame . . . is to believe that one's being is flawed, that one is defective as a human being.*"[6] Bradshaw calls this "toxic," because it poisons our existence. We have to live "on guard," in control at all times, lest someone expose us.

Shame is primarily cultivated in our early family-life experiences. Our primary care-givers are the ones who give us our core identity. This is accomplished by looks and words that tell us whether we are "good" or "bad"; secondly, by the

---

[5]Bradshaw, p. 7.
[6]Bradshaw, p. vii.

kind of time and attention they give, signaling whether or not we are *worth* their attention, which we so highly value and hunger for. But parents who are full of shame themselves are unable to give their children a feeling of self-worth. In fact, they often want their children to validate them—and unfortunately, the shame is simply passed on generation after generation. Shame begets shame.

Shame could be called a "family inheritance" because it is a secret sin and can't be worked out. "Stories of inherited shame uncover poverty resulting from bankruptcies, suicides, childhood deaths and accidents where the parents feel they were to blame (or were being punished), or secrets surrounding pregnancies, births, and adoptions."[7] Secrets in families may involve alcoholism or other addictions, abuse, adultery, past prison terms, illnesses—such as venereal disease—instances of abandonment, and racial shame.

In situations like these, parents practice what is called the "no-talk rule." That is, no one in the family is allowed to address the compulsive, harmful behavior. Rather, everyone is forced to protect it by silence. Shame buries itself deep, producing individuals who are bound by its power.

I have discovered in my counseling that unresolved grief is another breeding ground for shame. Sara's older sister, Becky, died when both girls were adolescents. Sara felt that Becky had been her parents' favorite, because her accomplishments netted the most praise. Becky had been a straight-A student and a cheerleader. Sara suffered "survivor remorse," feeling that her parents would rather she had died. She felt responsible to make up to the family all they'd lost, and at the same time felt woefully inadequate compared to the "legend" of her sister. She experienced a deep self-contempt from the shame of surviving her sister. She tried to become all that her sister would have been, but her life was marked by a desperate sense of striving and trying to prove herself.

Women like Sara, who feel they have to apologize for their existence or prove their worth, often become *rescuers*. In this role they may find a man who needs to be "helped," and then spend the rest of their life trying to straighten out his problems of alcohol, drug abuse, emotional instability, financial difficulty, or inability to lock into a stable, meaningful career.

---

[7]Fossum & Mason, p. 44.

If they can help or "rescue" him, they feel their life has meaning.

Whatever the cause, children raised in shame-based families are themselves the subjects of tremendous control. Some parents control every part of their child's life, expecting excellence in all things. This control is to "make up for" deficiencies the parent dimly feels. Others control by finishing their child's sentences, and constantly correcting thoughts and attitudes. These children grow up feeling ashamed of their true inner selves—which were not "good enough" to merit the parent's approval—and often cannot think or speak for themselves. Their lives are monitored by a little voice within that constantly criticizes: "I'm so stupid, no wonder I failed." "What an ugly duck. Who would ever ask *me* out on a date?" "I'm such a loser, I'll never get a good job." This "voice" becomes an intricate part of the person's personality and continues to reinforce the shame that began in the home.

Children from homes like these seldom get support from their parents. Gail, for instance, had a teacher who made her sit in a corner for most of the afternoon because she was caught talking to her friend. She felt terribly humiliated, but knew if she shared it with her mother she would hear, "How many times have I told you to keep quiet in school? You're such a *big mouth*." Children who learn that sharing shame will only bring a painful judgment, also learn to bury painful experiences. Thus, they never get rid of their shame.

A second source of shame is school and peer-group experiences. If a child comes from a strong, supportive family, she will be able to handle the little, daily humiliations that each of us experience in the world of growing up. If, on the other hand, she already feels shamed and humiliated from her home situation, these experiences will serve to reinforce the suspicion that she truly is flawed.

Since children need the love and attention of both parents, another cause of shame for some in today's society is growing up in a single-parent home. In many cases, the mother is struggling to make a living and hold herself together. A child may interpret her mother's lack of attention as something wrong with her. "The impact of not having one's parents' time creates the feeling of being worthless."[8] Thus a child can feel there is

---

[8]Bradshaw, p. 43.

something undeserving about her.

Another source of shame is any form of sexual or physical abuse. Both forms of abuse produce fierce shame in their victims, and this is maintained by secrecy. It has been estimated that there are about 60 million victims of sexual abuse in our society today.

Betty was subjected to an incestuous relationship with her father from the age of eight until she was sixteen and left home to marry. Her deepest hatred was not toward her father but toward her mother, who knew about the relationship but looked the other way. Betty felt the typical child's intense loyalty to her family and kept her secret, fearful that if she disclosed it her parents would divorce. But her sense of deep worthlessness led her into abusive marriages and adulterous affairs. When she came for help, she was thirty-eight years old and had been a Christian for six years. It took tremendous courage for her to expose the pain in her past, because she felt that by being "disloyal" to her family, she was "proving" how shameful and weak she was.

A related source of shame is a sexually charged type of emotional abuse in which there is no physical incest or violation; there is, however, an "emotional incest" at work. Often a father will bond with his daughter (or a mother with her son), using the child to meet emotional needs. There may be nothing *sexual* about the relationship, though it may lead to romantic fantasizing on the part of the child. In the deepest sense, the child's innocence is being violated by the parent's use of the child. The child is exploited, feels deep shame, but doesn't understand why.

Ellen grew up as "daddy's girl" and enjoyed the special attention she had from her father. She often sat on his lap and remembered having a "strange" feeling when he slowly stroked her arm. Many times they went for long walks together, and she somehow sensed that he looked to her for respect and encouragement, something he did not get from her critical mother. Ellen never viewed her father's relationship with her as abusive, but often wondered about her deep feelings of shame and worthlessness.

To add to the list of causes for shame, some women today suffer the tremendous pressure of a poor "body image." Our society is obsessed with physical perfection. Bo Derek, in the movie "10," presents women with an impossible ideal. Rather than see our bodies as unique shapes embodying our individuality, we are more apt to see them as a deviation from the ideal. I have never met a woman who was satisfied with her body. At the health club where I teach aerobic workout classes, every woman has a goal. We aren't taking aerobics classes just for our health or for the "fun" of it, we are trying to change our body's shape so we can finally love the person we see in the mirror. Somehow, many never reach that point.

Many women see their body as an enemy to be starved, over-exercised and "beaten" into an idealized image. Most women can remember the trauma of undressing in a high-school locker room, feeling too flat-chested, too fat, too skinny, or having "thunder thighs." We compare ourselves not to other "ordinary" women but to retouched photos of Hollywood beauties without one dimple of "cellulite." No wonder most of us dislike our bodies.

## The Fruits of Shame

One of the ways that shame manifests itself as control is in *perfectionism*. If I feel that I am intrinsically flawed and imperfect, then I will hide it behind an attempt to be perfect. In conjunction with this perfectionism is a haunting fear of failure. Sometimes it prevents a woman from accepting new challenges in life—for fear of being exposed as flawed. Parents who live with shame themselves encourage the super-achiever who will validate them. These children are admired and loved for their performance and achievements rather than for themselves.

A second fruit of shame may be a spiritualized perfectionism. Christianity attracts those who feel deep shame. Jesus' promise to grant His righteousness is a powerful draw to someone who feels flawed and defective. If a woman who has been shamed becomes open and honest and allows Jesus to heal and restore, her heart attitude and outward habits of response will gradually be changed. She will move away from doing good things to earn approval and acceptance, toward acting in simple obedience to God. But because a shame-based person is accustomed to hiding and covering her shame, she may use Christianity as another defense against others and against her own feelings of inadequacy. Sadly, these women become judgmental and critical, and try to control others, making them feel as shameful as they do. They project their shame on others to lessen their own anxiety.

Addictions and compulsions are a third result of shame. "When we address addiction in a family, we open the door to the family's shame."[9] The addiction may be to chemicals, to work, to food, to shopping or to sex, but the victim will never be truly free until she deals with the shame at the root of her behavior.

"Rage is probably the most naturally occurring cover-up for shame."[10] Rage protects because it keeps people away and it projects the shame onto others. Rage may show itself in the form of criticism and blame.

Jamie's mother felt shamed because she was overweight and had only a high-school diploma. She took her frustration out on Jamie by constant criticism: "Can't you do anything right?" Jamie didn't realize that her mother was projecting her own shame and worthlessness on her. They were both caught in the same negative cycle of thinking and behavior.

## Control: The Cardinal Rule of Shame

No matter what disguise shame wears, there is one cardinal rule that all shame-based people observe: "Be in control of all behavior and interaction."[11] The shame-based woman is a controlling woman. She must be in control of all interactions, feelings and personal behavior so she will never be caught off-guard. The greatest fear is that of being vulnerable, because this will open her up to more shame. Not only does the shame-based person have to control her own thoughts, feelings and actions, but she will also have the strong tendency to control the thoughts, feelings and actions of others. They must never be given the opportunity to embarrass her, shame her, or think badly of her.

My younger sister, Jeannie, did not realize until recently that her desire to control stemmed from a fear of vulnerability. As a result, it caused her to apply pressures within her marriage.

Jeannie met Ken when they were both in high school. She was a freshman, Ken a sophomore. They dated for three years,

[9]Fossum & Mason, p. 123.
[10]Bradshaw, p. 90.
[11]Fossum & Mason, p. 88.

and when Ken asked her to go to his senior prom she was ecstatic. She would be the first of her friends to go to the prom!

She went on a shopping expedition for the perfect formal with four of her girlfriends, and they spent hours discussing the way she would wear her long, curly blonde hair. One month before the prom, however, Ken broke up with Jeannie and took another girl.

Jeannie was shamed and humiliated. Her friends knew she had already purchased the beautiful pink dress, and Jeannie dreaded the thought of going to school and facing them. Three days later she began to suffer painful bouts of colitis.

Eventually, Ken and Jeannie did get back together and married. But Jeannie had changed. The sweet, vulnerable child—the baby of the family—with a wonderful sense of humor, now became somewhat guarded, only noticeable to those of us who knew her well. Her humor also changed. Instead of making cute little jokes, she seemed to delight in saying shocking things and off-color remarks, especially if they would embarrass Ken.

After marriage and motherhood, Jeannie's personality became more and more domineering. She and I became Christians about the same time. We learned that we were to respect and submit to our husbands, and we both were convinced. Jeannie was sincere about her desire to respect Ken, but she had difficulty accepting his decisions, especially concerning money and major purchases. She never seemed to approve.

Then came an eerie replay of twenty years before.

Lisa, Jeannie's oldest child and only daughter, also met her boyfriend, Rob, during her freshman and his sophomore year of high school. After three years of dating, they made plans to go to his senior prom. Unbelievably, Rob also broke up with Lisa about a month before the prom and took another girl. Like Jeannie, Lisa also developed colitis, but a more serious ulcerative form. The similarities were too remarkable to go unnoticed. So were Jeannie's "subtle" quips about men. One day in a telephone conversation, I asked Jeannie if she had prayed and truly forgiven Ken "from her heart" (Matthew 18:35).

"Well, maybe I didn't really mean it," Jeannie replied, "but Ken and I did pray together once, and he asked my forgiveness. I thought it was settled then. But I keep bringing it up in my mind whenever he makes me angry or upset. Maybe I still hold it against him."

Jeannie and I then prayed together, asking that God give her insight into the emotional and spiritual repercussions caused by her shame and resulting bitterness. She needed to clearly see what price she was paying by unforgiveness, and be truly willing to let it go.

In time Lisa and Rob also got back together and married. Things seemed to go well until Lisa got pregnant and became seriously ill again with ulcerative colitis. She had to be on high doses of prednisone, a cortisone derivative, with potentially serious side-effects. Jeannie was quite concerned about Lisa and her unborn child.

Jeannie and I agreed to fast and pray about Lisa's illness, and asked God to show Jeannie if there was still something left undone. Jeannie called me two days later to tell me that she had already received an answer to our prayers. She had awakened about 5:00 A.M. that morning and for some reason began to think about her very painful experience of rejection in high school. In the early morning stillness, God seemed to ask what she felt when Ken broke up with her those years ago. Immediately, she knew the answer—unbearable shame and humiliation. Once she mentally identified the emotion, she also experienced it: Her body flushed with the painful remembrance, her heart beat faster, she became nauseated and she felt absolutely worthless.

Standing in that place of utter honesty, feeling that core emotion of shame, Jeannie again prayed and forgave Ken for the humiliation he had caused her. She also asked God to help Lisa, if she had by words or actions passed on a bitterness toward men to her daughter that was contributing to Lisa's present illness.

As Jeannie shared her early morning experience with me, it became clear that she'd never been able to fully accept Ken's decisions or to respect him. At a deep level, she feared a repeat of the shame and humiliation she had suffered in high school by his rejection. Being in control was her "protection" against that happening again. Her jokes and put-downs were also a way of shaming Ken as she had been shamed.

Jeannie also asked Lisa's forgiveness for raising her in a way that transferred negative attitudes: "You must always be in control to protect yourself," and "When a man embarrasses you it is unpardonable." She had bequeathed to her daughter, unknowingly, a legacy of bitterness. Lisa in turn was responsible for her own inner housecleaning regarding her attitudes.

The outcome is that Lisa's health improved rapidly, and several months later she delivered a healthy baby girl.

Bradshaw says this type of toxic shame is "passed from one generation to the next."[12] Because shame is a secret emotion, it can't be worked out and so is multigenerational. Eventually, though, "all the secrets get acted out."[13] Perhaps this is what happened to Lisa: Her body acted out in physical pain, not only her mother's humiliation, but her own as well—a double-dose. Once it was out in the open, however, she could forgive and be free.

## Taking a Long Hard Look

Facing shame means that we have to face the feelings involved with the shame—even if it is hard to do. To fully accept the salvation Christ purchased for us with His death is to make choices that will free us from past experiences and long-ingrained habits. Of course this takes effort, and Paul encourages us to "work out your own salvation" (Philippians 2:12).

It was only when Jeannie was willing to relive the painful feelings she had suffered by Ken's rejection that she could *truly* forgive Ken "from her heart." Before exchanging her shame for Jesus Christ's grace, that relationship was shadowed and not "in the light" (see 1 John 1:7). Jeannie had tried to forgive Ken by a mental act, but she had reserved the right to hang on to her emotions about his rejection of her. True forgiveness is a work of the heart—the seat of our emotions. Jesus warns that unless we are willing to forgive from this deep level, we will be tormented. Often we would rather deny unforgiveness and cover it with an outer "spiritual" facade than to deal with the underlying pain. Sometimes it is only when we mothers see our shame being acted out by our children that we have the courage to let our true feelings surface so that we *and* our children can move toward freedom. This requires letting go of the facades by which we try to control others' opinions of us.

Proverbs 11:2 says, "When pride comes, then comes disgrace, but with humility comes wisdom" (NIV). Pride *will* ensnare us and keep us from revealing our shame; but if we adopt a humble attitude and confess to God, we will find healing

---

[12]Bradshaw, p. 25.
[13]Bradshaw, p. 32.

and will know *His* righteousness within us (1 John 1:9).

When Jesus hung naked on the cross, He carried not only our sin but the shame of that sin as well. Psalm 69:19, a psalm that foreshadows the coming of Christ, says, "You know how I am scorned, disgraced and shamed."

Isaiah 50:6 indicates of the Messiah: "I do not hide from shame—they spit in my face" (TLB). And Hebrews recounts that Jesus "was willing to die a shameful death on the cross because of the joy he knew would be his afterwards" (Hebrews 12:2, TLB).

How can we move from shame—from our self-justifying striving—to resting in God?

I suggest a first step of meditating daily on the wonderful truths presented in Paul's letter to the Romans, about our spiritual "position" in Christ.

> Now a righteousness from God, apart from the law [from our performance], has been made known. . . . This righteousness from God comes through faith in Jesus Christ to all who believe. . . . There is now no condemnation for those who are in Christ Jesus . . . (Romans 3:21–22; 8:2).

If God has stopped condemning us, now is the time to get on His side and stop sinfully condemning ourselves. Self-condemnation can masquerade as "holiness" because it gives us the feeling that we are "putting to death the self-life." In fact, self-condemnation is just another *self-effort* to be good enough for God.

The only way to replace old condemning lies that are buried in a wounded soul is to replace them with God's truth about who we are—to turn away from "self-consciousness" to "righteousness-consciousness." It means we stop trying to hide from God the sickness and sin in our souls and to freely say, "God, you know all about me. You know exactly how I will act and respond, unless your Spirit pours out your grace and strength upon me right now, at the moment of my weakness." For those who will turn to God, not when they are "strong" but in the moment of weakness and temptation, the beauty is that He *will* come!

He will not only help us escape from shame—but from the burdens of too much responsibility and from a "victim" mentality, which we will consider in the next two chapters.

*He who trusts in himself is a fool, but he who walks in wisdom is kept safe.*

*Isaiah 47:8*

# 9

## "It's All Up to Me"

Gloria and her husband, Ralph, are going to a dinner party. Ralph knows he'd better get out of the bedroom and give Gloria some space—and that it might be a long wait. She has already tried on five outfits and discarded each one in a heap on the bed. She's furious that she has put on a few pounds and complains that she is too fat to fit into her clothes. She's also upset that her hair didn't turn out the way she wanted. Ralph told her it looks great, but Gloria just glared as if he didn't know what he was talking about.

Ralph knows that other men think he's fortunate to have such a beautiful wife and one that keeps herself so impeccably groomed. He wonders what they would think if they saw her now. He loves Gloria but would like her to be less compulsive about her appearance.

Every time they go somewhere it's like Academy Awards night in Hollywood. She probably would have better relationships with women if she weren't so obsessed with her appearance. When they walk into a party, the other women eye Gloria with a mixture of admiration and jealousy. Ralph feels a little jealousy himself because most of the other husbands will be drawn to Gloria, and she'll spend the evening in conversation with them. Gloria always excuses this by saying she really doesn't relate well to women. Ralph is secretly ashamed and grieved that he and Gloria hardly ever make love, because it will mess up her hair or her makeup or her schedule.

Gloria, and many women like her, are over-achieving perfectionists. They control others and they are controlled themselves by compulsiveness. They seldom realize how deeply their perfectionism affects those closest to them. Inside they are most unhappy people.

The perfectionist receives her reward when someone admires her spotless home, mentions her slim figure, or compliments her appearance—but those rewards are only the bait that draws her into a control trap. She has to *continue* to strive for perfection, since she is hooked on the approval of others.

Through counseling, it was revealed that Gloria was scared to death that someone would see beneath her beautiful exterior the lack she felt within. Others, looking only on the outside, come to faulty conclusions: "If she keeps such a perfect house, she must be okay." Or "Anyone that perfectly groomed has to know what she's doing." Or "She's so disciplined in her eating. She's really on top of it all."

## The World's View

Why is it so easy to assume that keeping a flawlessly clean house, or being perfectly groomed, or having wonderful children, or having a great body means that we are acceptable and worthy human beings? My conclusion is that we are often swayed by the world's view of people and success. Even though we may be Christians, we have not *unlearned* old standards by which we gauge others, and by which we often drive ourselves.

How does this happen? To begin with, girls are often judged on the basis of their appearance, while boys are judged on the basis of physical prowess. Even fairy tales program us to believe that blonde or raven-haired beauties have it made, while the rest of us, the "mousy brownette" majority, must settle for life's leftovers.

We are also assaulted by advertising and movies which maintain the fantasy that beauty is the outward symbol of goodness and happiness. Studies done on college campuses some years ago found that "physically attractive people are perceived to be more sensitive, kind, interesting, strong, poised, modest, sociable, sexually warm and responsive, and outgoing than less attractive people."[1] Further, these studies

---

[1]Frank Greve, "For the Ugly, Life's Not Pretty," *Chicago Tribune* (Sunday, February 12, 1978), pp. 1, 24.

revealed that by the time children are six years old they have learned to differentiate between handsome and homely class-mates—and they do. Employers tend to pay homely people less; teachers assume that homely students are less bright, more trouble, and come from less-desirable families; jurors are inclined to find them less believable, and voters even think they are less worthy of high office. Chicago actually had an ordinance at one time that barred "diseased, maimed or *ugly*" people from public streets. A plastic surgeon, commenting on the hypocrisy of our society, stated, "We're the most cosmetic society ever on earth, but we still regard vanity as a sin."[2]

Like myself, you no doubt have noticed how the beautiful women of this world seem to get all the best. Perhaps you are one of the truly fortunate ones, by worldly standards, who have been able to sway people not only by your looks, but by what you possess or by your abilities. Outward attractiveness is equated with happiness and power, and studies reveal that physical appearance is a very effective way of influencing oth-ers—whether in competing for grades, a job or a spouse.

As Christian women, once we become aware of how we are influencing others through our outward perfectionism, we be-come accountable to God to change our behavior. Before we can change though, we need to clearly understand the "why" of our perfectionism.

## The Root of Perfectionism

Pamela always intimidated me—which was my problem, not hers. But what kept me at a distance was that she was too perfect.

One morning, as we visited together, I couldn't help but notice how perfectly her earrings matched her black and tur-quoise outfit. Her thick dark hair had that skillfully tousled look, accented by highlighted streaks. I automatically reached up to pat my hair into place—it looked just as tousled, but minus the professional touch. Why did I always feel like such a frump in her presence? And when I went to her home I felt even worse. Besides her eye for color and a flair for finding just the right accent piece, Pamela also kept a spotless home. She was gracious enough to have a little surprise gift for each

---

[2]Ibid.

visitor. I always left feeling like I'd just received an "F" in household management.

Today she had come to discuss *her* problem: She had just been diagnosed with a bleeding ulcer.

"There is no 'medical' reason for this," she said eventually. Then she ducked her head. "I guess I know in my heart that I keep myself under a lot of pressure. I'm so obsessive about everything having to be perfect. I just can't seem to relax and let things go. I'm driving my husband and kids crazy—and I'm killing myself."

That day I learned not only the reason for Pamela's perfectionism but a humbling lesson on judging by externals. Maybe if I had not allowed myself to be so overpowered by her apparent super-mom status, she might have confided in me *before* illness got her attention.

As we spent more time together, I learned that Pamela had been raised by an alcoholic mother. Her father was seldom home, and in Pamela's estimation he stayed away to avoid the problem. The care of two younger sisters fell to Pamela, and she often cooked dinner while her mother slept off her over-indulgence. Pamela also became the family "hero." A straight-A student and an overachiever, she was the "good" girl who would prove that her family was really okay.

While in college, Pamela had a brief relationship with a man and became pregnant. She went to live at an aunt's house for most of her pregnancy, then gave up the baby for adoption. The shame of her early family life and of the child born out of wedlock were still vivid, open wounds in Pamela's soul. Talking about them brought fresh tears, fresh pain.

Eventually we came to understand that much of Pamela's performance-orientation, which was eating at her, came out of her intense feelings of shame and guilt. Bradshaw notes that "super-achievement and perfectionism are two of the leading cover-ups for toxic shame."[3]

Our work together centered on helping Pam gain the assurance of God's forgiveness for her affair in college. She also asked the Lord to help her forgive her mother for her alcoholism and failure to provide the nurturing that Pam needed. She then had to begin the work of forgiving herself. It would

---

[3]John Bradshaw, *Healing the Shame That Binds You* (Deerfield Beach, Fla.: Health Communications, Inc., 1988), p. 61.

require a lot of deep inward searching, prayer and openness on Pam's part to reverse the toxic effects of her early life.

Since that encounter fifteen years ago, I have consistently seen how compulsiveness becomes a cover-up for some deep guilt or shame. Many books are written today about compulsive behaviors, and so I will limit my attention here to just one type of compulsive behavior—eating disorders.

## Eating Disorders

Signs of compulsive behavior that are dangerously on the increase today are *anorexia, bulimia* and *severe dieting*. A recent study discovered that the baby boomers (those born between 1946 and 1964) are obsessed with fat reduction. "More than half admit to constant dieting, and experts report an increase in the number of BBs diagnosed with bulimia and anorexia, syndromes once thought to be associated only with teens."[4]

*Anorexia* is a compulsive need to control weight by stringent dieting. *Bulimia* is a compulsive cycle of starving, binge-eating and vomiting. *Shape* magazine conducted a "Why Do You Diet?" study in 1988, and 95 percent of the 5,000 respondents were "very concerned" about their weight, even though most were only marginally overweight.[5] "A majority of respondents (81 percent) acknowledged that they felt self-confident and *in control* only when thin, and 62 percent said they felt '*most in control* of their lives' when dieting, regardless of whether or not they needed to lose weight" (italics added).[6]

Often, a woman with an eating disorder was the "good" girl in her family—the mediator who tried to control and hold the family together through overwhelming stresses, such as divorce, illness or alcoholism. She may have tried to make up to her parents for the failures of her siblings; she may have been one parent's confidante; or she may have struggled to please a never-pleaseable parent with her accomplishments. She may actually believe now, that if she controls her eating and her shape, she will be perceived as good enough to gain control over present problems in the family. In reality, her

[4] Lois Joy Johnson, "Grown Up," *Ladies Home Journal* (January, 1990), pp. 102–108.
[5] Peter D. Vash, "Why We Diet," *Shape* (July 1989), pp. 82–84.
[6] Ibid.

eating disorder only serves to mask the deeper problems, and will lead her to an early grave.

How did this over-emphasis on body-image as it relates to power come about? Let's take a brief look.

## The Women's Movement

During the women's movements of the 1960's, there was an explosion of interest in dieting and exercise. In the '60s, Twiggy, the stick-thin model, became the prototype of the new female figure. She replaced the buxom, curvaceous Marilyn Monroe as the sex symbol. Most of us saw the "Marilyn" types as helpless, powerless pawns of men; Twiggy represented the strong, independent, new woman.

It is not a coincidence that the emphasis on thinness and the women's movement coincide, in my opinion. As women assume more and more control in society, they have attempted to shed the weight that labels them "female." According to Brett Silverstein, Ph.D., associate professor of psychology at City College of New York, who studies the relationship between body ideals and culture, "Curvaceous women with large hips and breasts are thought of as less intelligent and less able to perform academically and professionally than their slimmer counterparts. With these stereotypes intact, it's not surprising that many career women will diet to deemphasize their feminine curves."[7]

Severe dieting, anorexia and bulimia are on the rise today because thinness is symbolic of strength, independence and achievement, as well as attractiveness. Also on the rise is weight-lifting for women. I have been a trained aerobics instructor for six years, and it is increasingly apparent that many young women prefer the very well-developed upper body musculature. Researchers at the Eating Disorders Clinic of the University of Cincinnati Medical College found that young women today are under great pressure to be thin and strong. "For the first time in memory, young women are expected to grow up to be more like their fathers than their mothers."[8]

The women's movement has also had a strong impact on

---

[7]Carol Jacobs, "Scuttling the Thin-Is-Beautiful Stereotype," *Shape* (July 1989), pp. 85–86.
[8]Susan Wooley, and O. Wayne Wooley, "Thinness Mania," *American Health* (October 1986), pp. 68–74.

"womanly goals." Girls and boys grow up very differently—girls have been traditionally raised to value relationships and form strong emotional bonds with their mothers. Boys are normally encouraged to compete and achieve. In today's world, however, "girls are being asked, in adolescence, to become suddenly like boys: to break the ties and become independent high achievers."[9] Young girls are also competing in sports like Little League and even asking to be allowed on football teams. Women feel they can no longer look to being a homemaker and mother, thanks to the women's movement, and feel they must have a career and become self-reliant.

The women's movement constantly exhorts us: "Take control of your life." And that really means—become like a man.

The anger and dissatisfaction that many women feel toward a caretaking role in society possibly has its root in a much older rebellion that took place somewhere back in eternity . . . when Satan rebelled against his assigned role in God's scheme of creation (Isaiah 14:13–14).

Satan was not content to stay in his designated role, and one of his main temptations toward the residents of earth is similar. To the woman, who is to be submitted to the man (1 Corinthians 11:3), his temptation is that she has more right to make decisions and rule over the man. Satan's first attack on the woman caused her to become dissatisfied with her position in the scheme of creation. If she would eat, then she could be "like God, knowing good and evil" (Genesis 3:5).

Today, women are bombarded with lies: *submission* indicates inferiority; *equality* means competition ("Anything a man can do, a woman can do better.") The bottom-line issue is being able to separate *personhood* from *role*. Yes, it is true women are equal with men before God (see 1 Corinthians 11:11–12), but we have been assigned a different role. That role is not my *identity*, only my function. All who are redeemed by the blood of Christ find their identity in Him, regardless of gender. Fulfillment in life comes first from contentment in the place God assigned to us.

The article on baby boomers that I cited earlier made an interesting point: "Even though we've all been exercising like mad for the past ten years, we still hate our bodies."[10] Of

---

[9]Ibid.
[10]Johnson, pp. 102–108.

course—our bodies are a reminder that we have been created to be the nurturers, the caretakers. Breasts especially are symbolic of this role. In severe eating disorders, a woman's breasts literally dry up and disappear and her menstrual cycle ceases. She loses what is particularly feminine and fits her for the role of nurturer.

Women who strive for perfectionism, whether in appearance, thinness, or in a spotless home, have fallen for several lies. Here are some basic wrong beliefs we have accepted:

- If I can just get thin enough I'll be happy and everyone will love me.
- I know I'll have a better marriage if I can keep myself looking attractive.
- I can atone for my past failures by being the perfect housewife.
- If I keep my house spotless, people will be more accepting of me, respect me more.

We women seem to hold on to child-like "magical thinking," that if I do "X" then "Y" will happen. We are the ones who read the self-help books, buy the latest wrinkle creams, become anorectic, submit to plastic surgery, visit the "fat farms," suffer liposuction, spend billions a year on cosmetics and feel that perfection is attainable. The drive for perfectionism, when it becomes consuming, has serious consequences in every area of life.

## Effects of Perfectionism

Perfectionism will affect us physically, emotionally and spiritually. As we have noted, physically, women have been driven to severe forms of dieting, anorexia or bulimia to achieve the perfect body. The world says, "You can never be too thin or too rich." But you *can* be too thin. Pop music star Karen Carpenter was when she died in 1983 from the effects of anorexia nervosa. Even the compulsive cleaner may drive herself to chronic fatigue in an attempt to keep her house perfect. This type of compulsive person is taxing her health by allowing that inner pressure which will never let her sit and relax or let down. This type of stress affects and depresses the immune system, lowering your body's resistance to many possible diseases.

Emotionally, the woman who is obsessed with her appearance or with the cleanliness of her home has difficulty finding meaningful relationships. Her focus is on the impression she is making and whether or not she is being rejected or respected. The competitive spirit can be a hindrance to relationships, since others feel that pressure to compete. But the quality of our life is determined by the quality of our relationships—with God, with others, with ourselves. If we are unable to sustain good relationships, we will most certainly not enjoy the abundant life.

On the deepest level—the spiritual level—the perfectionist misses the whole point of Christ's coming to the earth. He came *because we are not perfect*. "For all have sinned and fall short of the glory of God" (Romans 3:23). Perfectionists try to cover over their guilt of past sin or shame by being the best housekeeper, the best groomed, the thinnest, the most Bible-literate. But the perfectionist falls into the deception that her good works will cover over her failures past or present, when only Christ's atoning blood can cleanse away her sins and faults.

It is easy for the perfectionist to secretly feel proud of her self-discipline and control, and very difficult for her to let others see that she too has problems and is limited. For a woman like this, pride is a difficult sin to deal with, because change requires becoming vulnerable to others. To step down from a self-made pedestal and begin to share fears and insecurities with brothers and sisters in Christ is excruciating when one has worked so hard to get up on that pedestal, "above reproach."

When my friend Pamela was willing to trust me with her "shameful" past, it was the first step toward her being released from perfectionism. For the first time, I also felt close to her. It's hard to have a relationship with someone who wants to impress you, but when Pam was "real," our hearts were joined together. I had to become real with her, too, and confess my own sins of judgment and envy.

Once we realize how we control others and diminish our own self-esteem through perfectionism and compulsiveness, we are responsible to change. We will have to turn from our need for others' applause and commendation, to a desire to please God first. After all, vanity—whether in our appearance or in our home—is working hard to achieve an end that has no eternal value. The writer of Proverbs 31 has aptly stated: "Charm is deceptive, and beauty is fleeting; but a woman who fears the Lord is to be praised" (v. 30).

Instead of trying to impress others with our perfect-ness, we can refocus our attention on becoming more like Christ, putting on the godly attributes of love, peace and joy, (Galatians 5:22) that only come by abiding in the Holy Spirit. The Bible also commands us to be hospitable (Romans 12:13); but if keeping a picture-perfect home is our main goal, we'll never be able to create a warm and welcoming environment. Our goal as Christians is to be able to give our home and our possessions to God for His use.

Of course, as Christians, ours is a lifelong journey in spirit. But we can make our first significant steps when we forsake our preoccupation with externals, and begin allowing the Spirit of God to develop the character of Jesus within. Someday each one of us will discard our natural body as easily as a snake sheds its skin. It won't matter then if we have a perfect shape, our makeup is cleverly applied, we are wearing the latest designer outfit, or that we've kept the cleanest house in our neighborhood. The only thing we can take with us is the character of Jesus Christ that is formed in us by our cooperation with the Holy Spirit. What we have allowed Him to do in us is what we will have for all eternity.

As your sister in Christ, I encourage you to let your life's labor be for those things that never perish, for the "true riches" that come from living in union, more and more each day, with Jesus Christ.

For we know that life is not all up to us. We have a sovereign Lord who wants us to labor not for worldly supremacy, position, equality or adulation, but to enter into His *rest* (see Hebrews 4:1–11).

As we continue to explore the effects of control on us and on others, we will also discover how to cease our struggles, both inner and outer, and live in a state of well-being and rest.

*A man without self-control is as defenseless as
a city with broken-down walls.*

*Proverbs 25:28, TLB*

# *10*

# *"But I Can't Help It"*

The control technique we examined in the last chapter places women very obviously in a take-charge position. Now we will look at the kind of thinking that places some women in the role of "the victim."

Laura never had a weight problem until after she got married. Now, two children later, she can't seem to get rid of the extra twenty-five pounds she gained during her last pregnancy. Her husband, Sam, is constantly after her to lose weight and has promised her a new wardrobe if she can get down to her honeymoon size-10 figure.

But the incentive of new clothes isn't enough to motivate Laura. She feels overwhelmed by the constant demands of two small children and never seems to make progress on her daily chores. Her inability to get organized makes her depressed and she finds herself constantly angry at the kids. She's afraid of losing her temper and hurting the children, but has discovered that nibbling on something during these times quells her anger.

She knows that Sam finds her extra weight a sexual turn-off, but most nights she's so exhausted anyway that she just falls into bed. Laura still has plans to lose the weight and get back to a size 10, but at this point in her life she's just trying to make it through each day and doesn't want the added stress of dieting.

Laura, incidentally, is typical of a number of married

women. The authors of a new book called *Weight, Sex & Marriage* conducted a survey of about 25,000 women and found that "during 13 years of marriage, the average woman gained 24.7 pounds."[1] At the beginning of the survey, the authors assumed that being fat was never a choice, and were amazed at the number of letters describing "the usefulness of being fat and the pitfalls of being thin."[2]

Though Laura feels that she is a victim of circumstances beyond her control—children, housework, adult life-responsibilities in general—she has found an effective (if subconscious) way of controlling her husband's sexual advances—by being heavy and unattractive. She feels overwhelmed by her responsibilities and is all too relieved not to be pressured into sex.

Like Laura, many of the survey respondents, consciously or not, "put on weight to escape marital sex. Weight gain usually serves a double purpose: it diminishes a husband's sexual interest, and it inhibits a woman's own sexual desire."[3] Also, after the birth of two children, Laura might well fear becoming pregnant again. Many wives in the survey indicated that they used their weight gain as a form of birth control.

Another benefit of staying overweight is that Laura doesn't have to deal with her anger. Instead, she can swallow it with her food. Bradshaw found that obese people often become tied up in angry feelings. "Anger manifests itself in the gut (a tight gut), and eating and being full take away the feeling of anger by deluding persons into believing that their tight gut is about being full, rather than about the anger that needs to be expressed."[4]

Probably one of the strongest motivations to remain overweight, for some women, is the protection it offers against the fear of failure—after all, when you are overweight people might not expect so much from you. Cindy found that this was one of the major stumbling-blocks to her losing weight.

Cindy's problems began during her adolescent years. She went through an early puberty and was very well-developed

---

[1] Richard B. Stuart & Barbara Jacobson, *Weight, Sex & Marriage: a Delicate Balance* (New York: Simon & Schuster, Inc., 1987), p. 24.
[2] Ibid., p. 49.
[3] Ibid., p. 56.
[4] John Bradshaw, *Healing the Shame That Binds You* (Deerfield Beach, Fla.: Health Communications, Inc., 1988), p. 99.

even in the sixth grade. She disliked being teased about her buxom figure and was afraid of her blossoming sexuality. If she gained weight, she reasoned, she could hide behind it and not have to face the stares from the boys in school.

Finally she was 125 pounds overweight, and that was her excuse for not facing squarely her fear of failure. She would think, "Well, when I lose weight I will . . ." Or "If only I were thin I would . . ." Her weight protected her from doing the things she was afraid to tackle.

When a woman begins to use her weight problem as an excuse or to control others, she soon becomes trapped. She may suffer intense self-loathing because of her lack of control, she may become isolated in her home because she is embarrassed about her appearance, her self-esteem will certainly plummet, and if she works outside the home, she may have to settle for a lesser position because of her appearance. All these factors add another bar in the cage she has fashioned for herself. She thinks of her *weight* as her restrictor, when it is her *attitude* toward her weight that keeps her in bondage. She may eventually accept her imprisonment with no hope of escape.

This is not to say that all overweight women have become so because they have a victim mentality and want to use their weight to control or to avoid intimacy. But as already cited, it *is* a widespread problem, and it can lead a woman into a defeated position in which she feels desperate to regain some control and self-respect. When that happens it is all too easy to actually begin relying on the extra weight as a means of excusing yourself from unpleasant demands—or to avoid getting on with life because the weight becomes a prime focus.

Even the woman who is in Christ can easily get sidetracked into thinking, "I'll serve God better when I get this weight off. He can't really expect much of me in the condition I'm in." In part, this thinking is contributed to by others in the body of Christ who project an attitude of rejection toward someone "who can't even control their eating habits." But God's call to us is to serve Him *today* (Hebrews 3: 7–11), to come as we are, vessels fit for our Master's use (2 Timothy 2:21).

We should note that being overweight is not the only condition that can keep us believing we are victims, and therefore excused from the responsibilities of life and of service to our Maker.

# Proceed At Your Own Risk

The doorbell rang at 10:30 one morning, and Elsa made her way through the jumble of toys, newspapers, and popcorn bowls scattered over the living room floor. "Now who could that be?" she mumbled, trying to tuck her uncombed hair behind her ears.

On the doorstep was Gretchen from across the street. They were supposed to be getting together to plan the church supper for next weekend. "I'm so stupid," Elsa said, slapping her forehead. "I totally forgot."

The two women threaded their way into the kitchen. Elsa attempted to clear a space at the table, putting the dirty dishes into the already overloaded sink. Her baby was sitting in his high chair in an obviously dirty diaper, and milk dripped slowly onto the floor from his overturned cup.

"Excuse the mess," Elsa said weakly, pulling her bathrobe together, "I'm a little slow this morning."

Gretchen assured her that it was all right, but privately wondered why she'd ever agreed to work on a committee with Elsa, since everyone knew she was totally disorganized.

Perhaps you know someone like Elsa, or can yourself identify to some degree with her. It seems ludicrous to imply that Elsa derives any benefit from her scrambled approach to life. On the contrary, we would feel sorry for someone like Elsa who is so obviously overwhelmed by her responsibilities and who possesses few organizational skills. But perhaps this is one of the major benefits for a woman like Elsa—sympathy from others, as well as low expectations.

A woman who is unkempt and keeps a disorderly house is often trying to fend off pressure, so she controls her environment by ignoring it. She programs herself to think: "If my house is a mess, I can't be expected to entertain." Or, "Jason can't count on me to be his room-mother, I'm not even able to finish my work at home." Or, "I'd love to be able to accompany Walt on some of his business trips, but I'm so ashamed of my appearance. I just don't have the time or the money it takes to keep myself looking nice." Or even, "I'm so helpless, I just don't know how other women do it."

In the end Gretchen assured Elsa that she'd find someone else to help her plan the church supper, and apologized for bothering her. Ultimately, the woman who looks so helpless and out of control is really very much in control of others and her environment. Some of us (especially perfectionists!) find it difficult to see Elsa's state as a result of choices she herself has made. The Elsas among us effectively discourage anyone, including husbands and children, from asking anything of them, because we know they are so easily overwhelmed.

Whether a woman is using extra weight as an excuse, a slovenly appearance, an untidy house, or becomes a "victim" of illness, as discussed previously, she is controlling through indirect methods. Earlier we noted that women who control indirectly usually feel degrees of powerlessness. A woman in any of these situations is suffering from a "welfare" mentality. ("I can't take care of myself, so someone else has to help me.") She may have a very low self-esteem and feel terrible about herself; she may be quick to tell others that she is helpless or a "basket-case," but actually she could accomplish much if she would make an effort, one step at a time. It's merely become easier, though less and less rewarding, not to help herself.

When a person looks upon herself as a victim, she is not responsible for her problems. The "fault" lies with her mother, her husband, her metabolism, her children, her upbringing—something else has predisposed her to the problem. She would love to change, but . . .

Cary, for instance, said she really wanted to lose weight. She knew that her life would be more fulfilling and that her marriage would improve if she felt better about herself. Before I could assure her of my support and encourage her to get involved with other women in the church who are successfully losing weight, she went on to tell me why she was doomed to be fat forever. Since she had been sexually abused when she was young, she said, "I have to stay fat and unattractive to protect myself from men." Besides, she had three active children, and eating was the only way she could relieve the stress of caring for them. By the time Cary finished, I realized that she had built a prison of "reasons" around herself. She was no longer responsible to change, in her own eyes.

Deborah has always hated the shape of her face and her large nose. She doesn't feel that makeup would improve her appearance—so why bother? Betty's mother was an invalid and unable to clean house, so Betty never learned housekeeping skills from her. Now she's too embarrassed to ask anyone for help, because they'd see her messy home.

Each of these women carries one of the most crippling attitudes: *self-pity*, because of her predicament in life. Each thinks her lot is not due to her own failure, but rather to life circumstances or another person's failure. She sees herself limited by the injustices of life and overwhelmed by hopelessness.

The authors of *Weight, Sex & Marriage* offer advice that is helpful to anyone who views herself as a victim:

> We don't have a prayer of helping a woman who is overweight and overwhelmed unless we convince her to change her beliefs about her weight problem. She cannot allow helplessness to be her dominant emotion. And she cannot use the circumstances of her life, no matter how unfortunate, as excuses for her weight problem. As long as she thinks and feels like a victim, she'll act like one, and remain powerless over her body and her life. Only by accepting complete responsibility for her weight can she begin to change it.[5]

We may not always be able to control the circumstances of our life, but we can control our attitude toward the circumstances of life.

Releasing ourselves from the victim role requires that we correct our wrong thinking about our situation. Here are some wrong assumptions many of us live by:

- I have a sluggish metabolism, and will never be able to lose weight.
- I have to fix nutritious meals for my family, so it's impossible for me to diet.
- I get chocolate cravings at "that time of the month," and always blow my diet.
- I don't want my kids to think they can't enjoy their home, so I have to settle for a messy house.
- I can't afford to buy nice clothes, so I always look sloppy.
- I'm too busy to waste time fixing myself up in the morning.

Each of us could probably fill in our own examples of wrong thinking about why we can't lose weight, keep a cleaner house or present a more disciplined appearance. Instead of

---

[5]Stuart & Jacobson, pp. 85–86.

using the circumstances of life as an excuse, we can learn to take responsibility for our situation. It's also important to realize that as soon as we become aware of how we are using circumstances to influence others, we become accountable to change.

Once we realize that we do have a choice, however, we also may be tempted to blame our "basic personality." We might say, "I'm the kind of person who never had any will power, or personal pride, or ambition . . ."(or any other negative quality that keeps us from doing what we should do). We look to our past failures and reason that there is a deep character flaw that keeps us from being successful. Again, we take the defeated attitude that we are predisposed to this problem and can't do anything about it.

That type of excuse might work for a non-Christian. But Scripture says that "if anyone is in Christ, he is a new creation; the old has gone, the new has come!" (2 Corinthians 5:17). Not only are we new creations, but we have the indwelling power of the Holy Spirit: "And if the Spirit of him who raised Jesus from the dead is living in you, he who raised Christ from the dead will also give life to your mortal bodies through his Spirit, who lives in you" (Romans 8:11).

Good news! God *has* given us everything we need to have victory in every area of life.

It's true, therefore, that we need to carry our struggle to be free to a deeper level, getting past modern behavioral excuses to consider what factors are at work on the spiritual level that keep us locked into old, self-defeating behaviors.

## Seeing the Spiritual Truth

The first step for a woman who is caught in the trap of "helplessness" is to realize there is freedom in Paul's injunction, "Offer your bodies as living sacrifices, holy and pleasing to God—which is your spiritual worship" (Romans 12:1). We cannot be abiding in the Spirit of Christ if we are not submitted to God, even though we may be busy all the time with Christian activities. Cindy, for instance, saw that when she was not obedient to God in her eating, she did more church-related work to escape her sense of guilt. We can all fall into a religious trap—doing "our own thing," but putting God's name on it. Cindy came to realize that, for her, the kingdom of God was to be disciplined in her eating. Until she did that, her other activities were only in search of applause in one area to drown out the voice of conscience in another.

The woman who has offered herself to God will stop trying to control others by eliciting sympathy. Instead, she will learn to see herself as a disciplined ambassador for her Lord, no matter what her health, appearance or income level.

I cannot end this chapter without a few remarks about our *private attitude* toward our appearance and especially toward our bodies. As the national studies have indicated, even the most attractive woman is not content with her body structure or her facial features. Either her nose is too big, her ears stick out, her eyes are too close together, her hips are too wide or too narrow, her breasts are too large or too small, or her derriere is too flat or too round. We may be able to cover our facial flaws with plastic surgery and make-up skills, but we are more or less stuck with our body. Most women I know feel if they could only lose that extra ten pounds they would like themselves better. We have starved our bodies, then stuffed them and had to "go for the burn" in our exercise classes. We women run the risk of becoming obsessed with the shape of our bodies.

It is intriguing why most men don't have the same negative feelings about their bodies. A man can carry an extra twenty-five pounds around his middle and still be fairly content with his physique. But men *are* often obsessed with the woman's body, a common subject of art from the Great Masters to pornographic magazines. It is a known fact that a man's sexual drive is stimulated by the sight of a woman's body.

So it is the woman's body that goes through cultural evolution. The Renaissance women painted by the Old Masters were decidedly plumper than today's streamlined version, and we may be on the brink of another major change in cultural thinking. Jib Fowles, professor of media studies at the University of Houston, says that the stars we favor indicate social trends: "The fact that we have given Vanna White celebrity status is a key to seeing our society today. She's the harbinger of the reemergence of traditional feminine behavior. She's mute, obliging and servile. She's also busty, which is important. When family formation is important, as it was in the

1950's and is becoming so again today, we begin to see larger breast-sizes in our stars."[6]

Perhaps feminism has run its course and we will return to heart and home with traditional values. Obviously, however, the stability of that home must be based on more than a larger breast size. Perhaps our obsession about our bodies keeps us from realizing that what every man really wants from his wife, once he gets past the outer facade, is not a better body but "a gentle and quiet spirit." Peter tells us not to be overly concerned about outer beauty but "be beautiful inside, in your hearts, with the lasting charm of a gentle and quiet spirit which is so precious to God" (1 Peter 3:4, TLB).

If we are Jesus' disciples, then we will live in a disciplined, balanced manner, having control over our body and appearance, but careful not to fall into the obsessional body-image consciousness that pervades our society.

A better body will not make us happier—but a quiet spirit will, because it indicates a *trusting* spirit, just the opposite of a need for control. God says that this quiet spirit is "deep beauty" and attractive to the man. It's taken me a while, but I am willing to trust His opinion.

---

[6]Dan Hurley, "The End of Celebrity," *Psychology Today* (December, 1988), pp. 50–55.

# Section 4

# FAMILY TIES THAT BIND

*Better a little with the fear of the Lord than
great wealth with turmoil.*

*Proverbs 15:16*

# 11

# *Holding the Purse Strings*

Counselors know that finances spark more arguments among couples than any other subject. Finances themselves are only the battlefield, however, not the root of the conflict. In this chapter we'll explore this area to look at the real issues in the power struggle between men and women about money.

Personally, I never thought I had a problem with control in the financial area because John always paid the bills and made the major decisions concerning expenditures. Right after our honeymoon, John asked if I'd considered who was going to handle our money matters. Before I could answer he said, "I've decided I'll handle it." That was fine with me, because I absolutely loathed working with numbers. So for eighteen years John took care of all the bills and still gave me a lot of freedom with spending. Nor did I worry about our finances but trusted God to take care of us. So I was sure that this was one area in which I was completely submitted to God and to John—until the day John told me he might have to remortgage our house.

A wave of panic rose in me as John explained what was happening. He and four other Christian men wanted to purchase a fast-food restaurant from Hank, a new Christian in our fellowship. The bank was foreclosing on the restaurant, which meant that Hank would lose his home as well unless something was done. The bank insisted the restaurant could be purchased for half the price. But John and the other men felt that they should pay full price so Hank would be completely free from debt. There was no guarantee the restaurant would ever sell, of course. The alarming thing was that John was ready to re-mortgage our home—in which we had fifteen years of equity—to give us the necessary working capital.

Almost before he'd finished explaining, I nearly shouted, "No!"

John's eyebrows shot up at the intensity of my reaction. Even I didn't understand why I felt so panicked.

That night after everyone was asleep, I sat alone in the living room and asked God to show me why I felt so frightened. I sensed that it was rooted in something much deeper than the immediate situation.

After a time of prayer, a long-forgotten memory surfaced. During my childhood, we had moved frequently until my dad decided his family needed a more stable environment. When I was nine, Dad quit his traveling job and we settled near a small town in Pennsylvania, where we lived in a big yellow-frame house on an acre of beautiful wooded land. My sister and I spent hours playing house in a little clearing we made in the woods, catching crawdads in the trickling creek and swinging Tarzan-style on vines dangling from the trees. It was an ideal home life. But then my father's business failed, and he was forced to sell the house. We moved to a second-floor apartment in Chicago.

I hated Chicago. My resentment built, and I was angry at God, who in my mind allowed us to lose our home. I dreamed constantly about our two-story yellow house in Pennsylvania and the woods where I spent so many happy hours. If only we were back in that house, I reasoned, our family would be happy again!

Now, sitting alone in my living room in the quiet of the night, I felt once again all the pain of loss from that period in my life. Tears rolled down my cheeks. Mixed with the sadness was a lingering resentment toward my father for his business failure and the subsequent loss of our home. Underneath, I equated a house with happiness . . . so John's plan to re-mortgage our home tapped into this hidden well of anger and fear at the thought that we might lose this house, also.

To begin to sort it all out, I prayed and asked the Lord to

help me forgive my father for his failure. I also asked God to forgive me for my long-buried bitterness and anger toward my father—and also toward Him. Then I gave control of our home to God in a more complete way than I had ever done before. I told Him whatever happened I could accept it, because I knew my joy in life came from Him and not from our home.

As I slid into bed beside John, I felt a great peace in my spirit. Our financial strain did ease up a little after that, and we never had to take out a second mortgage on our home.

But the point is this: I was most surprised at how deeply the "money issue" was buried within me. I had prided myself on being "one of those women who doesn't think she has to take charge of the checkbook." I truly believe God used the restaurant incident to expose my hidden attitude, and to help me to release control of our finances to Him in a new and deeper way.

Today there are several schools of thought among Christians regarding married couples and their finances. Many believe that a husband needs to be in charge of all aspects of the finances, from decision-making to bill-paying. My husband and I believe that certainly a woman whose interest and skills lie in that area can balance the checkbook, pay the bills, and provide a second income if necessary. She should also be involved with her husband on personal investment decisions. But we feel that the *ultimate* responsibility for financial support should rest on the husband's shoulders.

So rapidly has society changed in the last generation that roles today are blurred and unpredictable. The advent of new and safe methods of birth control have given women a choice about pregnancy. The call to motherhood no longer governs a married woman's life, but rather her "biological clock" ticks off the fertile years. She chooses when she will become financially dependent on her husband as a determinant for becoming a mother.

Providing for the family has also changed radically. We no longer value "Arnold Schwarzenegger-type" muscles, except for esthetic reasons. A man's greater muscular strength and agility may have given him the advantage in primitive society and in heavy industry, but today's society has changed all that. The male is no longer "the prototypical industrial worker," and we have moved more toward an information society where the worker is "typically a woman." Mental work has replaced mechanical work and "in sheer numbers women dominate the information society—eighty-four percent of working women are part of the information service sector."[1]

*Megatrends 2000*, the book that predicts new direction for the 1990's, says that most of the new business leadership will come from women. The authors make the amazing statement that "to be a leader in business today, it is no longer an advantage to have been socialized as a male."[2] Already, "in finance women have reached the halfway point. More than half of all officers, managers and professionals in the nation's fifty largest commercial banks are women."[3]

It stands to reason that whoever has the economic power in a society will control the society. Likewise, whoever provides financially in a marriage controls the marriage as well. Power in our society is slowly drifting over to the side of the women who will have the edge in the '90s. God has established roles and in Genesis 3:17–19, as a result of the Fall, the main responsibility for providing for the family was given to the husband. Already we are seeing what happens when a society sets aside God-ordained authority and roles. The unprecedented divorce rate, homosexuality, and the abortion crisis reflect a changing society that has overthrown God-given structure.

Many women are not designed psychologically to handle the pressures of their family's financial responsibility. God gives us grace for those things for which He has given us responsibility. But as far as I can tell from scriptures such as Genesis 3:17–19, the primary responsibility for providing the family finances is the man's. If his wife unnecessarily assumes his role it can cause physically harmful stress.

Karen, a woman in her thirties, decided to go back to work to help pay some high credit-card bills. Since they had two small children, her husband Bob was not convinced it was a good idea. But Karen assured him that they'd be fine at the day-care center. Along with paying her train fare downtown, buying clothes suitable for her secretarial position, day-care fees and increased doctor bills because the children caught

[1]John Naisbitt and Patricia Aburdene, *Megatrends 2000* (New York: William Morrow and Company, Inc., 1990), p. 220.
[2]Ibid., p. 217.
[3]Ibid., p. 224.

sicknesses from the other kids, Karen had little to show from her paycheck at the end of each week.

"The biggest drawback, though," Karen told me, "was that before I went to work I really trusted God to help us in the financial area. I didn't spend much time thinking about money matters. I just thought it would be great to work temporarily and pay off our outstanding bills. Now I'm consumed with money problems. That's all I think about from the time I get up in the morning till I go to bed at night."

It is easy for a woman to become overburdened with financial worry if God did not design her to carry that burden on her own. Women have a special role in a marriage, and there is a very fine line between helping with financial matters and assuming full charge of them.

## The Marriage "Barometer"

Why do many men react in a negative way when a wife decides to go back to work, open her own private bank account, take over the family budget, or make major decisions concerning expenditures? I believe it is because they see these developments as violations of their primary role in the family—that of provider. If the woman takes over in this area, the man is left without a special and unique role in the family. "And one lesson that we can learn about male psychology is that men will not connect themselves for very long to families in which they are not needed. This is evident among ghetto families, where welfare payments serve the purpose of provider . . . The only group that has about as high a divorce rate as ghetto residents is that of highly successful career women."[4] For a marriage to enjoy its best success, the man needs to function in his God-ordained role of provider. The second reason a husband may react negatively when a wife attempts to control the finances is that she may be silently telling him, "I can't trust you to be in charge of the finances. I am going to remain in control, ready to be independent if necessary." When we unite in marriage, we become one flesh (Genesis 2:24) with our partner. To try to remain independent is to fight against the very union God has ordained. Until we are ready

---

[4]W. Peter Blitchington, *Sex Roles & the Christian Family* (Wheaton, Ill.: Tyndale House Publishers, Inc., 1984), pp. 61, 62.

to fully submit in the area of finances, our marriage will never come into the fullness that God intended. Instead of the combined strength of unity, we will remain two independent halves.

Dr. Peter Blitchington has made the observation that God made us so "we would need one another, and thus would grow together toward unity. By design, all of God's creation is constructed to avoid self-sufficiency."[5]

The bottom line of the financial war, hard as it may be to face, is that it is a barometer of our relationship with God. I realize there are a lot of women today who do not go along with my opinion that a man should be the ultimate provider. Many women are better at investment, wise purchasing, budgeting, and many have better potential as wage-earners because of natural gifts or training. There are others who were well provided for as young girls in their father's home, and it is difficult for them to settle for less while their husband slowly works his way up a corporate ladder. Still others, abandoned by a dad or a first husband, are afraid to relinquish financial control to another man who could also fail them. But ultimately, these attitudes indicate a basic lack of trust in God. It is easier to trust in our own ability than to release our control and trust God to work through our husband. There are also those Christian women who may say they have released the finances to their husbands but who still hold on by their inner chidings: "Why can't he remember to pay the electric bill on time?" Or "I wish he were a little more ambitious. He's never going to earn enough to support us." Or "I know so much more about budgeting than he does. I know I could do a better job." What effect will this lack of confidence have on him and on the family?

Let's look at what happens when finances become a central controlling issue.

## When a Wife Demands Control

In my case I didn't *want* to control the finances and pay the bills, but many women are more financially astute than their husbands and so they feel the responsibility to keep their family financially afloat.

---

[5]Ibid., p. 51.

Mary, for instance, was very good at budgeting. She borrowed money from her aunt to come to the States from Ireland, and within a year she had a good-paying job at the telephone company and repaid the loan in full. When she married Charlie, who was in sales, his salary was based on commissions. Mary made more money than Charlie and also took charge of the finances. Charlie often took the money leftover after the bills were paid and spent it frivolously. This only caused Mary to keep a tighter rein on the finances.

After Charlie and Mary gave their lives to Christ, Charlie began to learn about the responsibilities of a Christian husband and father. He decided he would take seriously his responsibility to provide for his family. Mary was very skeptical, since she knew Charlie could be impulsive and irresponsible. Often, when Charlie sat at his desk to pay the bills, Mary would call to him from the other room: "Don't forget to pay the electric bill!" Or "Check the telephone bill and see if it's accurate." Charlie would remind her that he was now taking responsibility and she should relax.

It all came to a head one summer day when they decided to take their three children to "Great America," an amusement park near Chicago. Charlie went to the bank to get $100 in cash. When he got home, Mary wanted to keep the money in her purse as she had always done, but Charlie firmly told her that he would carry the money.

When they got to the park, Charlie could not find the $100. As he frantically searched through his pockets, the Holy Spirit spoke to Mary about allowing her husband the main responsibility for providing for the family, and about asking Charlie's forgiveness for judging him to be irresponsible (which was exactly what she was thinking at the moment—"I knew I never should have trusted him with the money!") Right there in front of the ticket booths, Mary confessed to her husband that she had never really given up her self-reliance to him. She asked his forgiveness for undermining his authority in this area. Although they didn't find the $100, they did have some cash and credit cards, and ended up having fun as well as learning a good lesson.

Later that night after returning home, Mary was clearing the dishes from their hurried breakfast. As she bent to scrape the toast into the garbage, she saw the money in the trash. Somehow in the morning rush, someone had thrown it away with other wastepaper. She realized, in an instant of revelation, that this was symbolic of her attitude toward their whole financial status. She'd been certain in her heart Charlie would lead them to ruin. Her "chance" spotting of the bills seemed to her God's way of saying, "No matter who makes what mistakes, I can protect you." Also, her constant control and concern about money could eventually bring financial ruin. Scripture says it is possible to hold on too tightly and *lose everything* (Proverbs 11:24, TLB).

Often, when a woman is overly concerned about finances, she puts a subtle pressure on her husband to "do better." The pressure may be verbalized: "Can't you ask your boss for a raise? You know we won't be able to send the kids to a Christian school on your salary." Or it may come from a general atmosphere of dissatisfaction that permeates the home. That dissatisfaction will eventually contaminate the children who will also feel that Dad has failed them and they are missing out on things the other kids' dads can afford to buy for them. The pressure will either paralyze the man, or it will spur him on to be a workaholic.

It is possible that the man's provider role can become distorted so that the family views him as a walking vending machine. Whenever the kids want something, they just push the right button and out pops the money. Often he is not appreciated for himself, but for what he can provide. "The leech has two daughters. Give! Give! they cry" (Proverbs 30:15). That is all some fathers hear. A Christian father will have a deep desire to provide for his family and may feel he has failed if he cannot buy the extras. We can lighten the load by not demanding the latest, best and biggest.

Many men that I have talked to about this matter tell me that when their wife is overly concerned about finances, it tends to drain away the man's initiative and confidence. The wife's lack of trust can become a self-fulfilling prophecy. A man will be afraid to try harder for fear he'll fail and "prove" his wife's judgment of him. On the other hand, when the wife has confidence in him—better, trust in God in him—the man is able to function at his creative best.

## Real Security

Women often equate security with the husband's ability to provide, rather than with her heavenly Father's desire to care for her.

So do not worry, saying, "What shall we eat?" or "What shall we drink?" or "What shall we wear?" For the pagans run after all these things, and your heavenly Father knows that you need them. But seek first his kingdom and his righteousness, and all these things will be given to you as well. Therefore do not worry about tomorrow, for tomorrow will worry about itself. (Matthew 6:31–34)

If a husband is a good provider, it is sometimes easy to forget that God is the one who supplies. We begin to think it is our husband's boss that provides, or our own wonderful ability to manage finances that makes the difference. Spiritual complacency and ingratitude are often the result of this type of thinking. God wants our security to be in Him and not in our bank account. I believe He often will shake us up to get our attention. As Isaiah put it:

You women who are so complacent, rise up and listen to me; you daughters who feel secure, hear what I have to say. In little more than a year, you who feel secure will tremble; the grape harvest will fail, and the harvest of fruit will not come. Tremble, you complacent women; shudder, you daughters who feel secure! (Isaiah 32:9–11)

Because these women were financially secure, they had grown complacent. Complacency is a spiritual cancer that leads to death. To break them out of their complacency, God crippled them financially by causing the failure of the grape and fruit harvest. Then they realized they had taken God's goodness for granted and began to cry out to Him for their needs.

Agur, the writer of Proverbs 30, also understood the danger of being too financially secure when he prayed: "Give me just enough to satisfy my needs. For if I grow rich, I may become content without God" (Proverbs 30:8–9, TLB). Even though I didn't physically control the finances in our family, I did put my security in them. God used Hank's restaurant to show me my security was misplaced and also to show me that He could more than adequately provide. Even though we never had to re-mortgage our home, the restaurant did turn out to be a severe drain on our cash flow. Whenever John would mention that he had to put more money in the restaurant account, I secretly bewailed the situation. After all, we had only tried to help a brother in trouble and look how God had rewarded us.

In spite of my initial late-night prayer, worry about the future pressed at me—in two years, three of our four children would be in college. How could we possibly afford that when so much of our money was being absorbed by the restaurant? Then God did something that enabled me to more fully give my fear of the future to Him. He showed me how fully able He is to take care of our smallest needs—especially those over which we never think of extending our control.

We lived on a privately owned, small fishing lake. For the first ten years, our property was separated from the lake by a six-foot chain link fence. Then the owner decided to sell the lake to the village. Some time later, the village resold the property to the lake residents, and we took down the tall fence. Each resident was expected to maintain his section of beach, but we didn't have any extra money to put in the large amount of sand that was needed.

One day my husband received a phone call from one of his long-time dental patients. Dan was a Chicago policeman who had served a three-year prison term because of a civil-rights violation. His family could not receive any compensation during that time, and even his relatives deserted them. My husband had provided free dental care for Dan's family while he was in prison. In addition, John found people to assist them financially, and even arranged to have meat delivered to their home from a meat-packaging firm. Now Dan was out of prison and called to thank my husband for all he'd done for the family.

"So what can I do for you?" Dan asked.

"Oh, I don't need anything," John answered. But as they were talking, the subject of the newly acquired lake front came up.

"Do you need any sand?" Dan inquired.

John was almost too shocked to answer. Yes, we did need sand—tons and tons of it!

Dan told John that he was driving a truck for a company that hauled beach sand and he would like to bring us some as a thank-you. Two days later, Dan delivered one hundred tons of beautiful Lake Michigan beach sand, totally free of charge!

I realized that if God could provide free beach sand, He could certainly get our three children through college. It made me truly aware that all we have is ultimately from God, and I was able to more completely turn over my fear to God, even thank Him for the restaurant.

When Mary was learning to trust Charlie to provide the finances, little did she know that God was really preparing her to trust Him for all her provision. Just two years later, at thirty-eight, Charlie died unexpectedly of a heart attack, leaving Mary with three young children and very little money. Mary had already learned to give up her concerns about the finances, and now, eleven years later, she has seen God abundantly provide. She was able to buy a home near the church; when her car broke down she was able to get a new one; and two of her three children have already been able to go to college through gifts from other Christians. God's provision has stood the test again and again.

## Whose Principles Will You Follow?

What if a wife allows her husband to provide financially, and her irresponsible husband goes off and spends their rent money on a new motorcycle? A tough situation, obviously. Christianity seems to have degenerated into a "situational ethics" mentality. We respect Scripture and what it says when the conditions are right, then in tough cases we want to make up new rules. But there are families that really suffer because of the father's financial irresponsibility.

We often forget the power of God to change a person when we truly rest in the Word. Maybe that "irresponsible motorcyclist" is looking for a "vote of confidence" from his wife. (There are some good books as well as professional financial counselors to help with specific problems.) "The heart of her husband trusts in her confidently . . . so that he has no lack of *honest* gain . . ." (Proverbs 31:11, AMP). When a man feels the respect and trust of his wife, he in turn can trust her.

When the woman stops trying to control, she also helps to break the power of the curse hindering her husband's ability to provide that God issued at the Fall. This curse was the result of Adam listening to the voice of his wife and eating the forbidden fruit (Genesis 3:17). Jesus redeemed us from the curse of the law (Galatians 3:13), and *legally* it is broken, but we will not *experientially* see the effects until we women restore the proper authority structure in our homes. Adam *listened* to the voice of his wife and was cursed. Now it's time for wives to *listen* to the voices of their husbands and be blessed.

# Be Content

"But godliness with *contentment* is great gain. For we brought nothing into the world, and we can take nothing out of it. But if we have food and clothing, we will be *content* with that" (1 Timothy 6:6–8; italics mine).

"Keep your lives free from the love of money and be *content* with what you have because God has said, 'Never will I leave you; never will I forsake you.' So we say with confidence, 'The Lord is my helper, I will not be afraid. What can man do to me?' " (Hebrews 13:5–6; italics mine).

Many women have a hard time being content—blame it on our nest-building instinct. We want our "nest" to be fully equipped, and we want our little nestlings to have every advantage in life. The scripture from Hebrews indicates that as we learn to be content and trust God, we will be delivered from fear. The specific fear it refers to is a fear of the future. God assures us: "Never will I leave you; never will I forsake you." A person with a love of money will always have a fear of the future, but God promises that contentment will bring confidence about the future.

One of the most attractive qualities a wife can present to her husband and to the world is a contented and thankful spirit. This is far more appealing to a man than mere outward beauty. Contentment makes even a plain face charming. The wife who has learned to be content will be a wife who is appreciated. Then, like the wife of Proverbs 31, "She is a woman of strength and dignity, and has no fear of old age" (Proverbs 31:25, TLB).

God wants us to live our lives free from the love of money and free from worry about the future. In spite of my concern about my children's college education, three of them have now graduated. My oldest is now finishing his residency in Emergency Room Medicine without the debt that so many doctors have when they finish school. God provided all the money for his education through outside sources. My second-born, a daughter, is a lawyer. When God directed her to law school, He also provided a full-tuition scholarship.

In the final analysis, it's not so much the question of whether a woman works outside the home, pays the bills or figures out the family budget, but her *attitude* toward the finances. When the money is gone and there are still bills to be paid, do we panic and scramble to devise ways to get the extra money? Do we badger our husband or accuse him of being a poor manager? Or do we look to our heavenly Father? He "owns the cattle on a thousand hills" (Psalm 50:10), and He alone is the source of our provision. "The earth is the Lord's and everything in it" (Psalm 24:1).

God wants each of us to live in absolute dependence on Him to provide for all our needs. Trying to control and provide the finances and worrying about money only indicate that money is our security. God wants each of us to live with the exuberant trust of a small child toward her father. Our heavenly Father will never let us down.

*I have no greater joy than to hear that my children are living according to the truth.*

*3 John 4*

# 12

# *Children Under Control*

Kelly's face was animated as she told me about a Christian organization called Youth With A Mission (YWAM). Our daughter had written for information and was showing me the pamphlets she'd received in the mail. YWAM has mission bases all over the world, and her dad had given her the green light to go to the base in Maui, Hawaii, for the first stage in her training. I tried to look happy for her and nod my head at the right time, but inwardly I felt sick.

Kelly had just been diagnosed with Epstein-Barr virus (chronic mono), and I kept thinking, *No, this is the wrong time.* I knew I should be happy: I had a daughter who was committed to Christ and willing to sacrifice her time to spread the Gospel. For a long time I couldn't understand why I felt like something inside of me was breaking apart.

## Smother Love

A mother's bond with her children is one of the strongest on earth. Mothers often will risk their own lives to save their children. In the news recently, we heard about a mother who went to prison rather than disclose where she had hidden her daughter to protect her from what she claimed was a sexually abusive father. Mother love is a beautiful thing—but with

153

wrong motives, it can have crippling results in the lives of our children.

It is easy for us mothers to fall into the control trap when it comes to our children. Children are, after all, the fruit of our womb. For nine months we shared our body nutrients with them, put up with the discomfort of pregnancy, and then endured the pains of labor to give them birth. Perhaps because of this, mothers can feel they have a right to control and determine the life their child will live.

In the main, babies usually are Mom's responsibility. Often, there is little or no intervention from Dad during a child's infancy. In fact, many men are intimidated by a small, helpless infant and remain on the sidelines. A husband may also feel displaced by his wife's new "love interest" and feel jealousy toward the infant. Whatever the case, many women wind up with the majority of the child-rearing responsibility.

But often, her natural sense of duty is carried too far. A mother can assume the burden of every problem in her child's life and try to "fix" all the difficulties. If she is not able to make everything work out well, and smooth the way for her child, she may be consumed with guilt. Remember Alexandra, who was tortured by the conviction that she had transmitted hemophilia to her beloved son. She pampered and overprotected him in an effort to assuage her "blame." Modern mothers can be just as unreasonable in shouldering the burden for their children's lives.

Another way women can fall into a control trap is in keeping their children between themselves and their husbands. When the children are young the mother's whole life can revolve around bottles, formulas, diapers and feeding schedules. As her child grows, it is easy to make his activities the center of her life. The parent-child relationship soon replaces the marriage as the central relationship of the home. She may reason that her husband can look after himself, but the children really *need* her care and attention.

In extreme cases, there may be a role reversal in which a mother becomes dependent upon her child for emotional support. She will often make the child her confidante and share secrets with her that she does not share with her husband. These ties become deep and complicated.

We do live in fearful times and it is understandable why a mother today can suffer vague, free-floating anxiety about her children. She may have bad dreams, unexplainable panic, or find herself being highly critical of her children's friends and the homes of others where her children might go to play or spend time.

Each of these reasons for a mother's undue control can bring negative results in the life of the child, even the eventual rejection of, or rebelling against the mother. This, of course, is exactly the opposite of what she wants. The control trap also keeps a woman from experiencing the joy of mothering, and she is left anxious, tense and fatigued. The children who should be a delight become a burden.

Let's look more closely at each of the major reasons why mother love can smother. We will see how she can bring control into the right balance so that it becomes the measure of control that God intends—a means of giving godly direction.

## Right Start, Wrong Finish

*"I'm your mother—that's why!"*

As we have said, children live within their mother's body for nine months, and apart from the twenty-three chromosomes from the father, they are a product of the woman's body. It is our life-blood that circulates through the umbilical cord to the child and nourishes him. Even within the womb a bond is formed with our child that will not be broken by the cutting of the cord at birth. It is easy to understand why we mothers often see our children as extensions of ourselves—and, since they are extensions, we can subconsciously assume that gives us the right to control their lives.

But too often our natural "right" to control gets out of balance when we use it as a whip to drive and sting our children. Do you ever hear yourself saying things like:

"I walked the floor at night when you had colic, and now you think you can talk to me like that?"

"After everything I've done for you . . ."

"Since you act like a baby, I'll treat you like one."

"Don't you think I know what's best for you?"

The results are that a child will be frustrated or overly dependent because he is being held at the level of babyhood. Around the age of one year, a child begins developing toward independence physically, mentally, and emotionally. A mother's strong bonding to the child can serve as a bridge to help the child cross over into adulthood. She does this by encouraging, positive reinforcements and releasing the child at appropriate times to make his own decisions. Too much control limits a child's growth. This is one of the evils of control—not allowing him to develop into the person God intended.

Ours is never an autocratic right: Under God, our task is to raise children who know how to rightly respond to authority. One day they will have to respond to the laws of the land, teachers and employers, and of course, to God and His Word. Our function is to guide, discuss decisions, and teach a child to respect authority by our example of respect toward their father and toward other authorities. We are to help them learn from experiences both good and bad.

We tend to assume that we mothers always know what is best for our children. I certainly thought I did—after all, I was the one who spent the majority of time with them, who knew their strengths and weaknesses, likes and dislikes, attitudes and interests. Why, I no doubt knew them better than they did themselves! How hard it was, as they grew older, to stop "calling the shots."

When our second child, Shannon, was finishing her undergraduate work at Arizona State, she phoned home one evening to discuss what she might do the next year. I was about to tell her to continue on and get her Master's degree in English when my husband, on the extension phone, suggested she take the Law School Admissions Test.

*Boy, is he off the wall with that suggestion*, I thought. *Shannon would hate law school. That's the last thing in the world she's qualified to do.* But I kept those thoughts to myself as Shannon agreed to take the test. John said he would pray that God would either open or close the door to law school by the test results. I smiled to myself, because I knew the door would be closed. It was easy to submit to him, since of course he would turn out to be wrong.

About two months later Shannon got the results and she scored very high. In fact, she was offered a Dean's Scholarship to a law school in Chicago, which paid full tuition for all three years. To my great surprise, Shannon did have the aptitude for law school. And she loved it, was on the law review, had two articles published, and graduated cum laude.

This taught me a much-needed lesson. I may have a better understanding of my children's emotional needs, but I am wrong to undercut or overlook my husband's life guidance to our children. Men often have a better understanding of the "whole picture," while women tend to have the ability to fill in the details. The research on right- and left-brain functions backs this up: "In visual-spatial ability, males still hold an undisputed edge. The male advantage begins to show up around the age of eight, and persists into old age."[1] Since God ordained the man to be the head of his home, He certainly gives him the ability he needs to function as its leader. There may be some times when Mom does know best, but she also must move in unity with her husband when it comes to the direction of a child's life.

## "I feel responsible."

Modern psychology has fueled the myth that every problem in our life can be traced back to something Mom did wrong. Psychologist Paula J. Caplan says this type of thinking is "part of a widespread attitude of mother-blaming that surrounds us as invisibly as water surrounds fish."[2] She found that "mothers were blamed for causing more than seventy different kinds of problems in their children . . . Fathers were rarely blamed for their children's woes."[3]

It's no wonder moms feel so responsible. And Christian mothers are even more at risk because they have the strong desire to do things right and raise godly children.

Gail gets up early so she can give her children a nice, hot breakfast before they leave for school. (Do you ever wonder why moms consider "hot" to be so much more nutritious and "comforting"?) She also lays out their clothes the night before, so they won't have to make that decision in the morning. After school, she works with them on their homework and makes sure they have it done before dinner. Besides providing nutritious meals she also sees to it that they have enough time for play with their friends.

Last month when her oldest son's teacher requested a conference, Gail was shocked at what she learned. Eddie didn't seem capable of completing his school assignments, he wasn't

---

[1]"Men Vs. Women," *U. S. News & World Report* (August 8, 1988), pp. 50–55.
[2]Carol Travis, "How Psychology Shortchanges Mothers," *Psychology Today* (September 1989).
[3]Ibid.

participating in class discussions, and was somewhat of a loner. Gail was trying so hard to be the perfect mother and meet her children's every need. After long reflection and discussions with Eddie, she came to this conclusion: Eddie expected her to do everything for him; in "helping" she had actually taken away his motivation to do much of anything for himself.

The mother who feels too responsible is sometimes motivated by her own needs, not those of the child. She lives under the false illusion that she can ensure a problem-free life for her children, perhaps because *she* wants a problem-free life. Actually, she will deprive them of learning how to deal with life situations successfully.

## "If I left it to his father, it wouldn't get done."

It is true in many homes today that the father is either physically or emotionally absent and the burden of responsibility falls on the mother. These moms often struggle to fill both parental roles for their children so they won't be deprived. In too many homes, though, where Dad would like to be more involved, Mom intervenes between the children and their father.

The mother's role in the family can be likened to Jesus' role as intercessor (Hebrews 7:25). Just as Jesus is always interceding for us, so the mother is the one who intercedes for her children before God and before their father. But a mother may stand *between* the children and their father rather than "before," as a barrier rather than a bridge. How does this happen?

Let's say Dad is too laid back and easy-going. Mom becomes the disciplinarian. She doesn't expect him to discipline and set rules, and she takes over in that department. The result is that Dad will be slowly squeezed to the edge of the family and the children will view him as weak and ineffective. The children will be deprived of his possibly more tolerant and "big-picture" approach to life, which can be a perfect balance for Mom's occasionally heavy-handed authoritarianism.

In other instances, if Dad is too tough, Mom controls by being a peacekeeper, rather than a peacemaker. One of her methods is to selectively choose what she will tell Dad when he comes home at night. The mother serves as a filter in the home and strains out those things that she doesn't want the father to know. She may not tell him that Mary isn't doing her homework in science class or that Joey got into a fight at school. She stays in control this way, but her deception will harm the relationship between the children and their father and may instill in them a fear and hatred of authority. A filter can also become clogged, and the mother who practices this type of blocking will become spiritually "clogged" in her relationship with her husband and with God. She is walking in darkness, not in the light (1 John 5:1–7). She may even become physically ill, due to the stress of keeping the children's problems to herself.

Dad is too important a figure to be left out of the child-rearing equation. In fact, psychologists have now found that "fathers have enormous influence on the sex-role identification of their children . . . Fathers are major instigators where children's gender concepts are concerned."[4] It is the father also who gives a child a good self-image.

A mother's attitude toward the father may greatly influence the way the children relate to him, as my friend Patrice found out recently.

Christopher, her second child and only son, was very attached to her, but would never let his dad, Brian, kiss or hold him. One day three-year-old Chris called Brian "butt-head." Brian ignored it as a childish slip, but from then on Chris continued to call him derogatory names.

Patrice began to pray about the situation. One day, during her devotional time, she thought back to her pregnancy with Chris. It had been a very difficult period in their marriage. She and Brian had argued constantly, and the thought of a new life growing in that negative environment had made her tense and fearful. She resented Brian's lack of concern about her and felt he had abandoned her emotionally. As she remembered this turbulent beginning, she wondered if she had raised Chris with similar feelings toward Brian.

That evening, after the children were in bed, Patrice asked Brian if they could pray together about the situation. As they

4Glenn Collins, "Dad Plays Major Part in Defining a Child's Sex Role," *Chicago Tribune*, Tempo, Section 5 (December 26, 1984), p. 1.

knelt down by the side of the couch, Patrice realized that the past emotions of hopelessness, rejection and despair were not far beneath the surface—certainly not "long gone" as she'd thought. She realized she still had unforgiveness and resentment, and began to cry as she took Brian's hand. They asked each other's forgiveness.

Then they went into Chris' room and prayed for him. Patrice asked God to set Chris free from the effects of her resentment and asked God to give him a good relationship with Brian.

The next afternoon Christopher was in the family room playing with his little toy cars. Suddenly he came bursting into the kitchen holding a small, red truck and saying, "Mommy, look, this is like Daddy's truck!" Patrice knew that a healing had already begun because Chris never talked about his dad or related to himself anything he did.

From then on, Patrice began to work at correcting her own attitude toward Brian. It also required discipline to correct the bad habits Chris had picked up from her, *without her even knowing it*. Eventually, a restoration in the relationships brought Chris to a new love and respect for his father. What could have become a real disaster later, in Chris's teen years, was headed off.

## "But, Dear, I can't leave the baby."

A woman's nurturing nature is stimulated by the sight of a helpless infant. Most women are temporarily off-balance in the mothering department after the birth of their first child because of hormonal changes, and the sudden addition of such tremendous and mostly unexpected responsibility. Some women never get back to the central focus on their marriage. Instead, the child becomes a barrier in the relationship, physically or emotionally.

Clara's husband Tony planned a mid-winter vacation for them. The baby would be a year old, and Clara's parents were more than willing to babysit. But Clara refused to go and leave her child. "After all," she told Tony, "I've read that the bonding process isn't complete until eighteen months, so I can't leave him before then." In reality, Clara did not know how to relate to Tony anymore, and she used the baby as an excuse to avoid facing the cracks in their marriage.

Edna's daughter, Ashley, is eleven years old and shows great promise in ice skating. They've already made one move they couldn't really afford to be closer to the ice rink and to her coach. Edna's schedule revolves around Ashley's skating lessons, and her husband often comes home to an empty house and no dinner.

When a woman replaces the marriage relationship with her relationship with the children, serious problems are inevitable. It's difficult for a man to compete with his own children without looking selfish or immature. As a result, problems that develop in the marriage may be avoided, but they don't go away. Twenty-five years later, when the last child leaves home, the parents find they have no relationship. It is not unusual to see people divorcing after twenty-five or thirty years of marriage for this very reason.

The children will also suffer. No child likes to feel that he is the wedge between his parents or that he is the central prize in the power struggle between Mom and Dad. If forced into this place, he may feel divided in his loyalty and become double-minded in his thinking. When a child becomes the center of the marriage, he may also tend to think the spotlight should always be on him. The most devastating effect, though, is that the child begins to feel responsible for Mom's happiness, because of her misplaced emotional dependency upon him.

## "But I need you."

When a mother becomes emotionally dependent on a child, there are far more serious consequences in the long-run.

Karyn did not have a good relationship with her husband—in fact, she did not have a relationship at all. He was gone long hours from the home as a salesman and it seemed only natural that Karyn and her only son, Todd, would develop a very close relationship. Todd was the one who remembered her birthdays, wrote special little love notes on the calendar, told her she looked pretty when she dressed up for church, and held her hand when they went for long walks after dinner. She began to confide in Todd about her unsatisfying marriage, and his father's thoughtlessness. Todd always listened with sympathy.

Chances are good that Todd will be a weak, ineffective male who will most likely be controlled by his wife. He may even drift into homosexuality. Research has established that often the mothers of homosexuals "are too close to their sons, often encouraging an intimacy that should be reserved for the father only . . . Apparently this overly intense relationship between mother and son prevents the homosexual male from establishing a mature relationship with another woman."[5]

Even though this may be the extreme, a woman who is emotionally and sexually unfulfilled needs to be very careful that she doesn't look to her son to give her the emotional satisfaction she should get from her husband. This bonds her to the son in an unnatural way, and keeps him from having a strong relationship with his father. Without the father-son relationship, his self-image suffers, and he lacks assurance in his sexual role. If he marries, it can even become a wedge between him and his wife.

The effects of emotional dependency can be as devastating for a daughter. When Paula's parents divorced, her mother began to depend on her. She was seven, the oldest of three, and the most dependable. Her mom fell apart when their dad left. Now, at thirteen, Paula keeps the house clean, starts the dinner, and watches the younger kids until her mom gets home from work. Paula's mom often tells her how much she depends on her to keep things together at home.

Paula is already a very serious young lady—too serious for her age. She suffers from tension headaches, and often experiences overwhelming feelings of anxiety. Paula's future looks grim—she may become an overly responsible workaholic, unable to relax and enjoy life, and certain that everyone and everything depends upon her performance.

A mother who becomes dependent on a child does the terrible injustice of "stealing" that one's childhood. The parent is the giver and the child the receiver of parental love, attention, training and discipline. In the situations mentioned above, the roles are reversed and the mother receives instead from her child. Physical or emotional dependency, where the child is called upon to be parent to the parent, cripples a child by overburdening a young spirit with adult problems.

---

[5]W. Peter Blitchington, *Sex Roles & the Christian Family* (Wheaton, Ill.: Tyndale House Publishers, Inc., 1984), p. 141.

# "Mother will protect you."

A blackbird made its nest in a tree in my dog's run, and after the baby birds were hatched, she would dive down at my large Australian shepherd every time I let him out. Her desire to protect her young overcame her natural fear of a much larger animal. We mothers often feel that same fierce protection toward our young, and woe to anyone who causes them pain! Who has not seen an enraged mother fly at some person who was a threat to her child? Of course no mother wants her children to suffer failure or pain, but in an attempt to shield them from these situations we may be depriving them of valuable learning experiences.

In his junior year of high school, our son John joined the newly formed soccer team and was elected co-captain. The coach seemed to dislike John from the beginning and made his life miserable. Often he wouldn't allow John in the starting line-up—an embarrassment, since he was co-captain. The coach would yell insults at him when he was playing, and if John happened to be playing exceptionally well, he would pull him out of the game. What made it even worse was that John was the only one he treated in this manner.

One afternoon John, furious with his coach, came home from practice and told me about his latest humiliations. I felt very angry myself, but realized it could be a valuable growing experience if John could master the situation emotionally. My "comforting" words must have shocked him: "I think this could be a great experience for you, John," I began.

"A great experience? You're nuts! I hate it!" John shouted back, his face contorted with grief and anger.

"Think about it," I replied softly, sending up a silent prayer for wisdom. "You have been successful in everything you've attempted." (John was a straight-A student and he had many awards and many friends). "You have never had any disappointments in life."

"So what? Who wants disappointments?"

"Everybody suffers disappointments and frustration in life. It's part of growing up. If you never learn how to cope with them, you will be a pretty weak, self-centered person."

"So how do I deal with the coach's unfairness?" John asked, not too convinced.

"It *is* unfair. I get angry for you, too. But all of us will suffer unfairness sometimes. He's still the authority on the soccer field, and you can submit to him and pray for him."

"Pray for him! I don't even like him," John muttered.

At risk of sounding preachy, I took a deep breath. "The Bible tells us to pray for our enemies, not just for those we like. You'll find that as you pray for your coach, something will change inside *you*. This is one of those times, John, when you can really believe what God's Word says and act on it—or you can handle it your own way. I know it's not easy, believe me, and I've blown it myself many times. I'm just suggesting you try it and see what happens."

John didn't really believe prayer would help, but he agreed to try my suggestion. The coach never did change. He was just as mean and unfair to John at the end of the two years John played soccer, but John learned some very valuable coping skills that God knew he would need during his four years of college, four years of medical school, internship and residency, during which he was often confronted with frustration, pain and failure.

Only through trial and error do we learn life's lessons, and if we are Christians we know that our God is ultimately sovereign. So often, though, we moms try to protect our children from failure by discouraging participation in activities:

"Should you really try out for cheerleading? You haven't had any gymnastics like the others."

"I wouldn't run for class president if I were you. You know Tim will bully the kids into voting for him."

"Maybe you should wait another year before you try out for football. You're still on the small side to compete against those big hulks."

We may temporarily protect our children from failure but set them up to fail in future life situations.

Or perhaps we try to soothe our child's failure by excusing it or blaming it on someone else!

"I knew Miss Swanson would pick Darla for the part. She always was her favorite."

"If Mr. Thomas had explained things better, I'm sure you wouldn't have flunked the test."

"I know you wouldn't have struck out at the game if that pitcher didn't throw so wild."

We may be sincere in our desire to help our child, but this type of help won't build good character qualities in our children. The Bible makes it clear that all God's heroes suffered pain, frustration and failure. We need God's perspective for our children. If we have a general, unnamed fear for our child, it may be a clue that the child has taken too central a place in our spirit.

C. S. Lewis, in his book *The Great Divorce*, depicts a mother in heaven looking for her son who was "taken" from her by an early death. She is still angry and says, "I don't believe in a God who keeps mother and son apart." She begins demanding to see her son from an angel who tells her that she will only see him when she gives up her right to him. The angel adds, "Nothing can be yours by nature."[6] She winds up yelling she would rather have her son in hell with her than in heaven without her. Another character in the novel says, "That kind is sometimes perfectly ready to plunge the soul they say they love into endless misery, if only they can still in some fashion possess it."[7]

This is a shocking statement, and perhaps seems far beyond anything you or I would ever voice to God or even dare to consciously think. But it is the attitude of the heart that God sees (1 Samuel 16:7b). That fictional mother, like many of us, thought she loved her son, and even cried to the angel that she gave up her whole life for her son, but Lewis observes, "She loved her son too little, not too much."[8]

When we try to block God's work in our children's lives, our real heart attitude, whether we know it or not, is this: "God, I know what's best for my child and you don't. I cannot turn my child over to your care because you might do something to my child that would hurt me."

## The Tie That Binds

I had to face this attitude in my own heart when it came to releasing our youngest child, Kelly, to God's care on her mission trip. After she had been in Hawaii for several months, I was convinced I had truly "given up" to God on this issue. Then she called home to tell us they would be going to Bombay, India, for a three-month evangelistic outreach. I was

---

[6]C. S. Lewis, *The Great Divorce* (New York: Collier Books, Macmillan Publishing Company, 1946), p. 95.
[7]C. S. Lewis, p. 105.
[8]C. S. Lewis, p. 105.

stunned! I knew a little about the poverty and filth in India from missionary friends, and it was certainly not a place I would ever want Kelly to visit. But I also realized, by the intensity of my reaction, that I had not truly released Kelly into God's hands.

John and I had planned to go to Florida for a mid-winter vacation, but quickly made arrangements to go to Maui instead to see Kelly before she left for India. The night before we were to leave, I became violently ill. As I was thrashing around in bed, I had the strangest thought: *God is after my life!* I kept thinking of a scripture passage in Exodus. Moses was on his way from the desert back to Egypt:

> At a lodging place on the way, the Lord met Moses and *was about to kill him.* But Zipporah took a flint knife, cut off her son's foreskin and touched Moses' feet with it. "Surely you are a bridegroom of blood to me," she said. So the Lord let him alone. (Exodus 4:24–26, italics added.)

Evidently Moses had failed to perform the covenant sign of circumcision on his son, and could not escape a near fatal illness brought about by the hand of God until Zipporah performed this rite on their son. Since Moses was going to be in a responsible role of leadership, he had to show faithfulness to the covenant obligations inherited from Abraham. The circumcision should have been performed when the child was eight days old (Genesis 17:12), and failure to receive circumcision meant the boy would be "cut off from his people" (Genesis 17:14), and out of God's will.

As I thought about that incident, I felt God was saying that I had not cut the cord between Kelly and me. If I failed to do so, she, like Moses' son, would be unable to experience God's will for her life. I asked God to give me His grace to release her totally to Him because I knew I had failed to do it in my own strength. Then I woke John to pray with me. Now it was up to God to work His grace within me.

I was thrilled to see Kelly waiting for us at the airport, but my joy was snuffed out by concern when I heard that she was still experiencing the symptoms of the Epstein-Barr disease, though she functioned normally. She was determined not to let her illness interfere with her life, but kept up her schedule of work and classes, believing that as she walked in faith, God would heal her. Unfortunately, my faith wasn't at that level and all I felt was fear for her upcoming trip to India. I know my disapproval showed through.

Kelly was allowed to stay with us for the weekend, and the next morning she and John decided to go para-sailing. I rode in the boat as a passenger. It was a glorious, azure-blue Hawaiian morning, and Kelly looked like a picture on a postcard as she floated behind the boat, with her red and yellow parasail billowing against that perfect sky. As I sat in the boat and watched her drift higher and higher, I realized that the strong cord holding her to the boat was necessary to allow her to ride the winds. But, conversely, unless I cut my invisible emotional cords to her and stopped manipulating her life through my words and actions she would never be free to follow the wind of the Holy Spirit. Again I prayed that I would let her go.

In fact, all I did intermittently for days was cry and pray. Evidently I had the flu, and it weakened me enough that my emotions, usually well under control, were all on the surface. John said that I cried more in those five days than I had during our whole twenty-seven years of married life. I knew God was allowing my fragile physical state so He could do His surgery, but I tried not to let Kelly see my concern or tears so that I wouldn't undermine her decision.

On Monday morning, Kelly had to be back at the mission base. Late Tuesday we drove out to join the group for their evening service. As we were singing songs of praise to God, Kelly was standing so close to me that I could feel her elbow against my side. "All right God," I finally surrendered, "I give her back to you. If you want her life—whatever you want to do with her—just let her bring glory to you."

I had a tiny indication of what Abraham felt when God told him to sacrifice his only son, Isaac (Genesis 22:2). But I also felt a tremendous lift—a sense of joy and lightness. I realized later that my crying was finished, much to my husband's relief. But more important than a change in my emotions was the change in my will. I had stopped worrying over *my* agenda for Kelly's life and committed myself to *His* plan for her.

Often, it is the very thing we fear most that is the issue we will need to face in our child's future. The mother in *The Great Divorce* was told she had to release the right to ever see her son before she could see him, and I had feared that Kelly would die in India, so I had to specifically consider that possibility and put her in God's hands. I had been haunted by the thought of Kelly's death and attempted to fight that as simply a lie of Satan. But it was always there on the perimeter of my mind. Now I had the opportunity to come to grips with it and begin a new kind of bonding with my daughter—one where she was free to listen to God's voice and obey Him without my intrusion.

The experience of release that I had in Maui was, in many ways, subjective. It happened within me. I didn't fully realize the spiritual transaction with God that had taken place until we received a phone call from Kelly several weeks after we returned home.

"I don't know what happened when you visited here, but everyone says I'm totally different now," she told me.

"How are you different?" I was really interested, because Kelly didn't know what had happened in me during the worship service.

"Before your visit I wasn't very happy about going to India. In fact, I wasn't even sure I wanted to stay in missions. But now I love it. It's like I've finally accepted God's will."

Had I somehow conveyed a more settled, joyful attitude about her choices, giving her a sense of confidence she'd lacked? Or was this purely the working of the Holy Spirit? There was no way of knowing for sure, of course, but I silently thanked God for His faithfulness and went on to tell Kelly of my experience.

That was not the end of the story, though. God had to help me live up to my commitment months later when Kelly was in India and became severely ill.

Kelly's own great fear had been that she would get sick while in India and I wouldn't be there to nurse her. During the five days she was ill, she made a decision to trust God and resisted the desire to call me. On the fifth day, she began to complain to God. She told Him that when she was sick at home I gave her ginger ale, crackers, and chocolate pudding, but all that was available in Bombay was highly spiced curried foods. The next day, a friend from another mission group dropped by to see how she was doing. He brought with him a small bottle of ginger ale, some crackers, and a can of chocolate pudding!

Later, when Kelly related the incident to me, she said with conviction, "Now, does God take care of me, or what?"

Kelly had been my most fearful and dependent child because of my over-protection of her. This experience was the completion of my releasing control of her, and her releasing dependency on me. Our God is so faithful, and once we yield our children to Him, He will bring them into maturity and use even our mistakes in parenting to bring good into their lives.

Kelly was a different person when she returned home. She was no longer my "baby," but a young woman with a new-found faith and trust in God. I doubt that this would have happened if I had grudgingly sent her off with misgivings about her decision.

God is patient, and He will not grab our children back to himself. He gives them to us to nurture and guide, but desires that we freely give them back to Him. Only in that way will they find His will for themselves.

Psychiatrist M. Scott Peck speaks to a daughter about her controlling mother: "It is the task of parents to assist their children to achieve their own independence and separateness. In order to succeed in this task it is essential for parents to tolerate their own loneliness so as to allow and even encourage their children to leave them. To discourage such separation not only represents a failure in the parental task, but a sacrificing of the child's growth to the parent's own immature, self-centered desires. It is destructive."[9]

We moms have a tremendous responsibility. God gives us children to nurture and raise to be responsible, godly adults. The exercise of legitimate authority and discipline will build self-confidence, but the illegitimate use of control will destroy self-confidence and produce fearful, insecure adults.

We are not perfect mothers, but God has a wonderful promise: "Love covers over a multitude of sins" (1 Peter 4:8). We know that God's love can cover our mistakes, and even turn those weaknesses in our children into strengths (2 Corinthians 12:9-10).

---

[9]M. Scott Peck, *People of the Lie* (New York: Simon and Schuster, 1983), p. 147.

*A worthy wife is her husband's joy and crown;
the other kind corrodes his strength and tears
down everything he does.*

*Proverbs 12:4, TLB*

# 13

# A Woman's Power Over a Man

Alex was stuffing the last of his afternoon's work in his top desk drawer when his secretary buzzed him on the intercom. The "big boss" wanted Alex in his office.

He felt his stomach muscles tighten. Two employees had been laid off that week. Alex entered Mr. Carr's office with an apprehensive feeling—but the big smile on his boss's face immediately made him relax. Mr. Carr went on to say that Alex's cost-analysis of the Fischer project caused him to make a major change, and as a result the company was netting an additional one and one-half million dollars above revenue projections this year. On his way out the door, the boss slipped an envelope in Alex's hand and said, "This bonus is well-deserved. And by the way, we're considering opening a new department. You're my choice to manage it."

Alex could hardly sit still on the commute home as he kept replaying his boss's encouraging words. He bounced in the front door like a winning quarterback after the Super Bowl, and handed his wife the envelope. While she was opening it he told her what his boss had said.

Her only comment was, "It would be nice if you'd work that hard around here."

The power of our words is truly amazing. Months of hard work, a raise, and a promotion can all seem worthless and pointless after a remark like that from the one who should share the joy and reward of such good news.

While it is true that some men are workaholics and ignore the needs of their wife and home, it is the rare person who benefits from negative criticism. It is easy to imagine Alex's shrinking, revolting feeling, all his excitement drained away in an instant.

Conversely, a man's worst day can be soothed by a woman's gentle words: "I really appreciate the way you work so hard for us and put up with all the stress on your job to provide us with this comfortable home." The words are almost unimportant compared to the appreciative spirit, which has the capacity of lifting a man instantly.

We women have more power over our man than we realize. My husband once told me that he could receive all sorts of accolades, but if he came home to an unhappy, disrespectful wife, they would all be meaningless. Ultimately a man wants the respect and support of his wife. If he has her confidence he can face any trial in life and overcome it. If he *doesn't* have her support, he will never feel truly successful.

## The Source of Our Power

Why does a woman wield such tremendous power? Even if she thinks her husband ignores everything she says, the truth is, her influence with him is great—and she is using that influence all the time, even if she doesn't realize it. The following are six ways a woman's power with a man shows itself.

*Intuition.* Women have known for years what recent right-left brain studies have revealed: We are more intuitive than men. Intuition, according to the dictionary, is "a direct perception of truth, fact, etc., independent of any reasoning process."[1] It drives men crazy when we say, "I don't know *how* I know, I just *know*." We seem to be blessed, or cursed, with the ability to see *into* a situation or a person.

A woman can see *into* her husband's mind and personality, and may at times know him better than he knows himself. He is shocked and caught off-guard when he is confronted with

---

[1] *The Random House Dictionary of the English Language* (New York: Random House, Inc., 1971), p. 747.

the frightening realization that someone knows him in this way.

Dan, for example, came home night after night discouraged and depressed because of the remarks of his superior at the ministry where he worked. One night after supper, he and his wife Becky remained at the table to finish their coffee and talk about the situation. "You know, Dan," Becky said gently, "your boss is an angry, sick man, but the longer you take his remarks to heart, the sicker you'll become. You're letting his words become true of you."

Dan was astounded by her statement, but he immediately saw the truth. He knew that Becky did not want to hurt him, only to help him get free. They began to discuss the boss's favorite put-down remark: "You don't know how to submit to authority." Becky pointed out that some of the things Dan's boss wanted him to do could get the ministry in trouble with the IRS, which Dan knew, and that as a Christian, Dan did have a higher authority. Dan's boss also accused him of being "young and aggressive"—which was true, but not in a negative sense. Becky helped Dan to see that his youth and aggression were really tempered by a deep commitment to Christ and were not ungodly.

Becky's explanation of these points and others had the power to bring Dan to his senses and get him out of a situation that was literally making him sick. He was amazed that she knew him so well and saw the situation so clearly. With her encouragement, he left that job and found work with another Christian organization whose business ethics matched his own high standards and where his drive was applauded and well-channeled, not put down.

Becky used her power of intuition *with wisdom* to help her husband get free from a discouraging situation. That same power, unfortunately, can also be used in a negative way.

Sherry knew that her husband, Bill, felt he was better qualified than his immediate superior at work, even though he never mentioned it to her. She used this knowledge as the tool to goad him into dissatisfaction, constantly nagging him to ask for a raise. "You do most of the work for nothing. Make them pay you what you're worth." Bill thought that if he did his best job with a humble spirit, God would reward him with a promotion in due time. Instead, spurred on by Sherry's comments, he began to reveal his dissatisfaction and a superior attitude, which threatened his supervisor. When the company had to make cut-backs, Bill was fired at his supervisor's request.

*Past failures.* A woman's insight lets her know where her husband is strong and where he is weak. She soon learns how to dodge his strengths in a conflict and to capitalize on his weaknesses. If he is logical, like most men, she avoids logic because he can "out-logic" her. Instead, she may use to her own ends his inability to be sensitive or in-touch with the needs of the children. "You just don't see how this decision will hurt me and the children, do you?"

I knew that my husband felt guilty about the fact that, in his opinion, he was not able to spend enough time with our children between his dental practice and pastoring of the church. So when I wanted to win an argument about the kids, I would say something like, "Well, you're *never* around, so how could you possibly know what [he/she] needs?"

That statement also revealed my resentment for past failures. We wives are often tempted to use mistakes from the past as a way of convincing our husband that he should listen to us now. "If you had only listened to me when I told you . . ." John never liked to get in an argument with me because he said I had total recall of all his past failures.

Some of the power women have with men comes from dredging up past failures and weakness, automatically robbing them of the respect, power and authority due them in the present.

Often we are not even aware how much events from the past influence our life. I certainly didn't see that the Thanksgiving morning John and I began to argue. He withdrew into the living room and I followed right on his heels, reciting my litany of grievances. As I walked behind him, it almost seemed that I stepped "outside" myself and observed what I was really doing. In a rare moment of self-revelation, I believe the Holy Spirit showed me that I had never forgiven John for *any* of the past hurts in our marriage. God's spotlight on my unforgiving heart cut my words short. John turned around in surprise, to see what had ended my tirade.

"John," I almost sobbed, "I've never forgiven you for any of these past hurts. Will you please forgive *me*?"

John's face showed his confusion at my abrupt change of attitude, but he was only too willing to offer his forgiveness.

When you and I release the past to God, we also release the power to control our husbands. Since that day, ten years ago, I have been aware of the weapon of using past failures and weaknesses against my husband. Because I no longer berate him for his lapses, John is more willing to communicate with me. Many women complain that their husbands will not share with them their innermost thoughts, including weaknesses and fears. Of course not! Why would they want to add ammunition to our arsenal? "Most women have an intuitive, primitive sense of exactly how to castrate a man when they are angry. Men know this, and appreciate it when a woman refrains from using this most deadly weapon, especially when they know they are wrong."[2]

*Heart-goals*. A woman knows what her husband's "heart-goals" or motives are, and she can either help him in accomplishing his goal, or block him by setting up obstacles. We have the power to either influence our husband for good or for evil, and we must use it carefully. We also must be careful not to *judge* our husband on the basis of his goals.

For instance, a man may seem to be preoccupied with appearances—nice clothes, the house, his car. But perhaps the deeper need of his heart is for *recognition*. If he receives the recognition he needs at home from his wife and family, he may be less likely to seek recognition on the basis of earthly possessions. Or perhaps you are concerned because your husband appears to seek power and position. He may be motivated by a deep insecurity. Ask God to show you how to help your husband feel more secure, and pray for God's enabling for his release from this inner bondage.

My father was a workaholic. He grew up in a poverty-stricken family, and from the age of fifteen was out on his own. He "pulled himself up by his bootstraps" as far as business was concerned. I never remember my mother complaining about his long hours at work. She freed him to do what he needed to do, because she knew that his heart motive was to provide well for his family. One of his major goals in life was to leave each of his children an inheritance. My mother not only allowed him to work, but also supported his goal by being a thrifty homemaker and not demanding luxuries.

My husband's greatest heart-goal as a pastor is to keep in

[2]Dr. Toni Grant, *Being a Woman* (New York: Avon Books, 1988), p. 87.

close contact with each one of his "sheep." For years I hindered this, because I often resented the countless phone calls and people who showed up unannounced at our door. I am more of an introvert, and felt overwhelmed by all the people; maybe even a little jealous, because my husband is a very approachable pastor. Most of our arguments were over this issue. I would quip that he wanted to be with the people because he was "nosy." Though I would say it in a joking way, he knew I was serious.

One night at church, John left me alone as usual in the front, and walked among the congregation during the worship time. This was a sore point to me, because I felt a pastor should remain in the front of the church during worship. As I was feeling more and more irritated, the thought came to me that John was milling through his flock, checking on his sheep. He would pause with a word for one, pat another on the shoulder, smile at another. As I watched him, I saw his beautiful love and care for the sheep and realized how fortunate I was to have such a compassionate husband. The children and I had certainly benefited from his gift. I was ashamed when I remembered all the times I had tried to block John from this God-given goal, and I asked God's forgiveness and His help in supporting John. Later I told this to John and asked his forgiveness as well.

*The "inscrutable" woman.* Men have been told since they were little boys, "You'll never understand a woman." It is easy, then, for a man to distrust his own abilities to understand women and be sensitive to their needs. The feminist rhetoric about wanting a "sensitive" man has added fuel to this myth. Consequently, many men live their lives thinking, "There's a whole world of inner laws, sensitivities, and understanding going on inside this mysterious female creature—and I'll never understand it." Some women love to capitalize on this myth and use it to their advantage.

For some time Terry and Peter came to John and me for marriage counseling. They had been separated for six months, but wanted to work through their problems because both were Christians and did not believe in divorce.

After several months of counseling, we felt it was time for them to pray and ask forgiveness of each other for specific hurts. Peter, in a very honest, sincere, and humble way, confessed his sin to God. Then he turned to Terry, taking both her hands in his. Through tears he said, "Terry, I ask your forgiveness for all the times I hurt you." He named specific instances that had come up in our counseling sessions, each time saying how sorry he was.

Terry's mouth began to quiver and turn down. Soon tears were running down her cheeks. I expected her to say, "Yes, I forgive you." But instead she said, "You just don't know how much you've hurt me! I don't know if I *can* forgive you!" With that she dissolved into sobs.

John and I exchanged "what now?" looks over their bowed heads, and I repressed a very strong urge to shake her. The impropriety of that tactic obvious, I took her aside to talk privately. By this time she was aware of her own failures in the marriage, and I reminded her that we can't receive God's forgiveness if we refuse to forgive others (Matthew 6:14–15). In the final analysis, I could see she didn't want to lose the power she had over Peter because "he just doesn't understand how deeply sensitive I am and how he hurts me all the time."

This "inscrutable woman" power that keeps a man "in the dark" about "how we women work" really doesn't fit with the openness and honesty of Christian love. The apostle John tells us that if we walk in darkness with each other we actually deceive one another and destroy fellowship (1 John 1:16). To keep the "fellowship," the companionship, in a marriage, it is the wife's responsibility to let her husband know when he does something that offends. She can do this best by assuming his motives are right even if his judgments may have been wrong.

She can say, "I know that you didn't mean to hurt me when you made that joke in front of my parents about my cooking, but I am very sensitive about that. I feel very inferior in the cooking department, and I was hurt by that remark." This approach does not accuse (which puts a person on the defensive) but requires that a woman humble herself, exposing her vulnerability. Most men become very protective when a woman admits to a weakness, especially when her spirit is humble and she honestly desires to bring reconciliation.

Most of us, unfortunately, expect our husband to know our needs, and reason as follows: "If he loved me he would know." And when he doesn't know, we move on to the next "logical" conclusion: "He doesn't love me." Husbands want to care for us and meet our needs, but they are not mind readers. They aren't particularly intuitive, and can't help if we don't tell them what our needs are.

When John would ask me what I wanted for my birthday or our anniversary, I would usually say something like, "Oh, you don't have to get me anything. I know money is a little tight." Of course, deep down, I expected him to see through this ruse and realize that I wanted that beautiful red angora sweater I'd seen in the department store. Naturally, I didn't get the sweater. I got candy ("Doesn't he know I've been dieting?"), or flowers ("Doesn't he know they'll be dead in three days?").

Why are we women so afraid to be honest about our feelings and desires? Are we ashamed of our needs, or do we want to keep the upper hand over men by keeping them guessing?

*The weaker sex.* We women know that most men will limit their power, because women are the weaker vessel. From the time he is very young, a male is exhorted not to punch, tackle or elbow-in-the-stomach a girl. When big brother finally gets baited by his little sister's incessant teasing and pops her one on the nose, *he* is the one who gets punished and little sister barely scolded. He soon learns that he is the strong one. To a man this can mean: "I must bear all the hard jobs, and keep my emotions to myself, expecting nothing of my wife, because she's not strong enough."

A woman's power emerges when she falls into the trap (as we saw earlier) of playing on sickness, weakness, and anger—knowing a man is afraid to hurt her. The sad truth is that while some men will resort to physical means, the majority will let a woman's weakness control them. Gordon Dalbey, speaking about a man's fear of women, writes: "Certainly, we men do not fantasize before *Playboy* centerfolds because we are so courageous before real-live, three-dimensional women, but rather, because we fear them; we do not beat up women because we are so strong, but rather, because we feel so powerless before them; we do not impregnate women and leave them to consider an abortion because we are so self-reliant, but rather, because we feel inadequate to be responsible fathers and husbands."[3]

Women need to understand the fear that a man has about a woman's fragility. If she uses it as a power to control him, it can drive him even further away.

---

[3]Gordon Dalbey, *Healing the Masculine Soul* (Waco, Texas: Word Books, 1988), p. 21.

Rob, for instance, just found out that his company is going to send him to San Diego, California, for a seminar. They offered to pay his wife's airfare also, so they could make it a mini-vacation. But Rob knows that Jana will never agree to go because of her fear of flying. It makes him angry that this will be the third trip they've missed together because of her fear. He remembers how attracted he was to her fragile personality when they first met, because it brought out his protective side. That's getting pretty old now. Every time he tries to firmly insist she go, she starts crying and tells him how he's upsetting her. It makes him feel powerless, and he's beginning to think he made a serious mistake in marrying her.

*A man's sex drive.* It is a known fact that most men have a stronger sex drive than women, and often a woman will use this as a lever of control over the man in their intimate relationship. The husband will avoid conflict if he knows his wife will resist intimacy with him later, or because of unresolved problems act put out at his advances, forcing him to back off.

When a woman wants to feel loved she wants to be held, touched, and reassured with words rather than sex. When a man wants to feel loved and comforted, he receives it through the sexual act. This may be because men "often express themselves sexually when they can't express themselves emotionally."[4] Little boys are raised to be tough and *macho* and the adult male has a hard time expressing vulnerable feelings. If your husband has had a bad day at work and comes home fearful that he is going to lose his job, rather than sit down and tell you how he feels, he may simply turn amorous. A woman, of course, may sense her husband's fear and anxiety, which will not incline her toward sex. She would rather sit and talk about his feelings of fear or inadequacy.

When a woman uses her power over their intimate relationship to control a man, it can make him "feel wrong, bad, dirty, embarrassed, and judged to be more unrestrained than she is . . . It also makes a man feel like he isn't good enough— if he were a 'real man,' he would be able to make her *want* him."[5]

The sexual act is a man's most vulnerable area. It is the act by which he "proves" himself; and his basic self-image is

[4]Barbara DeAngelis, *Secrets About Men Every Woman Should Know* (New York: Bantam Doubleday Dell Publishing Group, Inc., 1990), p. 128.
[5]Ibid., p. 165.

at stake. When a woman uses a man's sexual drive against him, she is really destroying her husband and the very fabric of their marriage. Paul reminds us, "The wife's body does not belong to her alone but also to her husband . . . *Do not deprive each other* except by mutual consent and for a time, so that you may devote yourselves to prayer. Then come together again so that Satan will not tempt you because of your lack of self-control" (1 Corinthians 7:4–5, italics added).

I have been surprised at how many Christian women who come for counseling "deprive" their husbands in direct disobedience to this command. When a woman has not submitted her sex life to the Lordship of Jesus Christ, she can even become "religious" as a cover-up. Because of this, they put their husbands in the dangerous position of being tempted by Satan. This is not to say that a man's lapses into immorality are always the fault of his wife. It is simply a reminder to all of us that we *dare not* put our husbands in jeopardy by using sexuality as a weapon, rather than a means of deeper unity.

## More Power Than Satan

From the beginning, women have had tremendous power with men. After Eve ate of the forbidden fruit, she gave some to her husband who, the Scripture says, "*was with her*, and he ate it" (Genesis 3:6, italics added). It is possible that Adam was standing right next to Eve when she succumbed to the temptation. Satan engaged Eve with the question, "Did God really say. . . ?" (Genesis 3:1). It seems clear Eve had the perfect opportunity to go to Adam and ask him to answer Satan's question; instead she decided on her own that God must not have meant what He said.

It is interesting to note that Satan did not directly approach Adam. Is it possible he knew that Eve had more influence over Adam than he did?

What *power* Eve had . . . Adam knowingly (1 Timothy 2:14) traded paradise rather than lose her. Satan must have known that Adam would listen to his wife rather than him, and he used this same tactic with Job.

When Satan approached God about Job, he argued that Job only feared God because of the blessings in his life. Satan said if God took Job's blessings away, he would "curse you to your face" (Job 1:11). So God granted permission, but Job remained righteous. Satan's next accusation was that if he was allowed to afflict Job's body, he would "curse you to your face" (Job 2:5). So Satan afflicted Job with boils from head to foot and still he did not curse God. Finally, Satan sent in his greatest weapon . . . Job's wife. "His wife said to him, 'are you still holding on to your integrity? *Curse God and die!'* " (Job 2:9, italics added). Job's wife said to him just what Satan said to God!

I shudder to think how many times I have allowed myself to be used to attack my husband when he is already discouraged or confused. I reluctantly confess that in the past I have been like Satan's messenger to John. Only when I began to understand the tremendous power I have over my husband did I develop a holy fear of that power. God has placed us in a role of great influence over our husbands, and it can be used for godliness, or it can be used for selfish ends.

We have a choice.

*Selfish or Self-less?* No doubt all of us are guilty at one time or another of using our power with our husband for selfish ends. We may play on his weakness, lack of competence in an area, or his fears. Our desires may also come out of our own fear, anger or shame, and we try to pull our husband into that trap with us.

We may use our position of power to nag our husband about his weaknesses, to embarrass him by revealing his flaws, or to go behind his back to someone else to try to get *them* to influence him. If our motivation is selfish, we will find ourself in the same trap as Eve, and most often we'll live to regret the fruit of our ungodly actions.

On the other hand, we can use this position of influence to help our husband achieve godly ends. That beautiful gift of intuitive sensitivity that God has given us can be used as we pray and intercede with God for our husbands. Though we may have insight into our husband that we are not at liberty to share with him, we *can* bring those insights to God in prayer.

Moreover, we need to ask God to show us our husband from *His* perspective so that our prayers are more merciful. Some wives love to pray "get-him" prayers, but they fail to realize that they will also be on the receiving end of those prayers.

There is an interesting story in the Bible (1 Samuel 25) about this type of situation. Abigail was a "beautiful and intelligent woman" married to a "surly and mean" man named Nabal. Nabal insulted David, and David intended to get revenge by killing him and all his men. Now Abigail could have said: "Good, now God is going to 'get him' for all the misery he's caused me." Instead, she interceded for her husband before David and brought him gifts. David was so moved by this woman's intercession that, later, when Nabal suffered a stroke and died, David took her for his own wife.

As wives we often fail to realize what it means to be "one flesh"—that what affects our husband will affect us also. Instead of praying those "get-him" prayers, we need to follow Abigail's example and pray for mercy and blessing on our husband.

We can also bless our husband by showing our loyalty and trustworthiness. One characteristic of the wife of noble character in Proverbs is that "her husband can trust her . . . She will not hinder him, but help him all her life" (Proverbs 31:11, 12, TLB). The wife who desires deep communication with her husband will have to show him that she can be trusted with his most secret fears and failings and will not use them against him.

Pam and Robert were at the office Christmas party talking to several couples when the subject turned to hunting. One of the men was going hunting over the vacation period, and he was telling about a deer he'd shot last year. Pam jumped into the conversation with the comment, "Oh, Robert hates hunting. His dad took him once and he threw up when he saw a dead rabbit." There was a little shuffling of feet and a bit of polite laughter, but the other men were definitely uncomfortable. And Robert seemed to draw into himself; he vowed never to tell her anything ever again.

What does the wife do, though, if her husband is about to do something she feels strongly about? Does she use her power to manipulate him into her way of thinking, or is there another way?

God has given women the power of appeal, and Queen Esther used this power wisely. Esther was a Jew who had been chosen to be the wife of King Xerxes of Persia. Xerxes was tricked into signing an edict to destroy all the Jews on a certain day. Esther was urged by her uncle, Mordecai, to appeal to the king for mercy. This was a dangerous step since anyone approaching the king without being summoned would be put to death—unless the king extended his scepter. Esther's appeal illustrates the godly way a woman can use the power of appeal she has with her husband:

1. Esther had the right attitude toward the king. She had deep respect toward him and toward the authority God had given him. It is useless to appeal to our husband when we do not submit to his authority and position of headship that God has given him. If we make our appeal in a despising, self-righteous manner, nothing will be accomplished. Remember, a man can sense when his wife is resistant to him, and will either overpower her in an attempt to break her will, or he will withdraw.

2. Esther spent three days fasting and praying before going to the king. Our appeals can be more effective when they are preceded by prayer and submission to the will of God. Someone has said that prayerlessness indicates an independent spirit. We can cultivate the godly habit of praying before our appeal, so that we are less likely to be trying merely to get our own way.

3. Esther was willing to sacrifice herself for her request. We need to have that same spirit of sacrifice. If, for instance, we want our husband to spend more time with the children, it may mean he won't have the time to do needed repairs around the house. We need to be willing for the trade-off.

4. Esther waited for the right time to present her petition. She held two banquets for the king and didn't give her request until the second. In between the first and second dinners, God prompted the king to dig out some old records, and he was reminded through them of how Mordecai, Esther's uncle, had once saved his life. This predisposed him favorably toward the Jews the very night before she presented her request. Our timing is also crucial and shows our submission to God's will.

5. Esther was honest and straightforward in her request. Rather than try to manipulate our husband into doing what we think should be done, we need to be completely honest. That means giving accurate information, without "loading" our words with emotions. For example: If Rodney needs extra help from his dad with his math, his mother should tell her husband about the teacher's report on Rodney's areas of weakness and how they can be strengthened. It would be manipulative to imply that Rodney is not doing well in math because Dad doesn't spend enough time with him. If that is her hidden

feeling, it would be better to present it in honest, mature conversation, without using the emotionally loaded issue of Rodney's poor school showing.

What if your husband fails to respond to your appeal? You can accept his decision in the right spirit—that is, in *faith* that God will work, even through a poor decision. A man dislikes failure and will often learn more from failure than any other way. Because he also longs for the admiration of his wife, he wants to be successful.

Lucille tried to persuade her husband Peter not to go into business with a neighbor. She disliked the man, but had no facts on which to base her feelings. Several years later, the two men reached an impasse in their relationship and the partnership dissolved, at quite a loss.

Lucille never said, "I told you so!" But Peter learned to listen to his wife's counsel and trust her intuition. This has drawn them closer together in their marriage, and Peter really values Lucille's insight and feelings.

Realizing the power that we have as women should bring us to a godly fear. Long after our children have forgotten the details of what took place in our home, they will remember Mom's *attitude* at the time. Was she quietly confident that God is ultimately in charge, and that "in all things God works for the good of those who love him" (Romans 8:28)? Or was she worried and fretful, keeping a tight reign of control, silently indicating that God really cannot be trusted?

The short book of 1 John gives us a wonderful principle that can be expanded into many areas of life: "If anyone says, 'I love God,' yet hates his brother, he is a liar. For anyone who does not love his brother, whom he has seen, cannot love God, whom he has not seen" (1 John 4:20). In the same way, if we do not trust the human authority given to our husband, how can we ever learn to trust the higher authority of God? The principle is always, "from natural things to spiritual things" (1 Corinthians 15:46). And those women who cannot trust God probably have never learned to trust the human authorities that God has put into their lives.

It would be wonderful if all marriages were examples of mutual submission (Ephesians 5:21), but we know that reality seldom represents the ideal. Many women will live their entire lives in less-than-perfect marriages. But more important than winning the daily power struggles in a marriage is keeping the spirit of unity. Unity provides the rich, fertile soil in which to grow strong, self-confident children—one of the great purposes of marriage from God's point of view.

Some may argue that when their husband changes, they will change. This is to neglect personal responsibility, and also to assume that we have the power to change someone else. Only God can do that. Remember Alexandra, who tried to mold Nicholas into a more authoritative monarch and destroyed the monarchy forever in Russia.

Women have tremendous power either for good or evil. The evil use of power is through control and domination. It is to reach out and grab the apple; to usurp the man's leadership in the home. But women also have the power to restore what was stolen, by submission to give back the authority of headship. We women can reverse the effects of the curse on Adam and his descendants. We will set our families free from the effects of that curse and come into a oneness that is like the relationship of Christ and His Church.

Now that's real power!

# Section 5

# SPIRITUAL ROOTS AND RELEASE

*The one who prophesies—who interprets the divine will and purpose in inspired preaching and teaching—speaks to men for their upbuilding and constructive spiritual progress and encouragement and consolation.*

*1 Corinthians 14:4, Amp.*

# 14

# *The Ultimate Trap*

Probably one of the toughest battles we will fight as Christians is the struggle between trusting God completely and taking matters into our own hands. When we ask Jesus into our life, we become "a new creation," a new person (2 Corinthians 5:17). This person wants to be submitted to the Father's will. But a war between the Spirit of Christ and our flesh—our natural inclinations and habits—begins. Each one of us fights the battle to trust and to relax in God's arms.

If we have the tendency to control, one of the most dangerous traps we can fall into is feeling that we know God's will for another person. Control then puts on a spiritual mask, and is much harder to recognize—and to escape.

My friend Elaine and her husband Craig, who pastor a church in Arizona, found out just how destructive spiritual control can be. I'll let her relate the story that led to its discovery:

> Craig and I had been pastoring a small church of about 200 people for several years when a beautiful young widow, Clara, began attending. Just three months after she had become a Christian, her husband was killed in a car accident. I felt deep compassion for her since she was such a young Christian and had already faced such tragedy. We quickly became friends and spent a lot of time together.
>
> She was a gifted woman, deeply religious. I really admired her, and felt my walk with God was somewhat ordinary in contrast to her intense spiritual experiences. The

189

only thing that bothered me about Clara was that she always said God told her what to do exactly, step by step, and that everything always worked out perfectly. When anyone in our small home fellowship offered advice to Clara, she would politely listen with a smile, but never really accepted counsel. "I'll have to pray about that," she would say. That was reasonable—but I wondered why she resisted our concern and help.

That summer we spent a lot of time together, and sometimes while we sat on the front porch sipping cold lemonade, she would question me about the responsibilities of a pastor's wife. Often she would interrupt my answers with a question like: "Do you think Craig really understands the stress you're under as a pastor's wife?" Or "Craig isn't very sensitive to the emotional needs of the congregation, is he?" I always defended Craig, but little doubts about his abilities were beginning to creep into my soul, turning into irritation.

Eventually, those doubts erupted in criticism and dissatisfaction with Craig. I often struggled with a fear of failure myself and had always depended on Craig's strength. But as I began to focus on flaws in his character, I became overcome with fear that we were not capable of pastoring a church.

Clara said that she prayed for us daily. Sometimes God would speak to her about His direction for the church. She wanted to share her discernment with the elders, but said they were probably too prejudiced against women to receive it. I spoke to Craig about some of her suggestions, which seemed visionary to me, but he just brushed them aside. This angered me, so Clara and I decided we would meet to pray that Craig would see the truth.

Several months after we began our private prayer sessions, I began to experience severe abdominal pain. This was diagnosed as a spastic stomach muscle. The doctor gave me the test results, and followed up with a little lecture about not taking life so seriously and learning to relax. On the way home from the doctor's office I did some introspection, and realized that my tension was connected to the growing inner struggle and resentment I felt toward Craig. That tension and the marital discord we were experiencing was a direct result of my agreement with Clara over Craig's shortcomings.

I began to understand that Clara's questions and negative observations had planted doubt and fear in my mind.

My agreement with her against Craig yielded a harvest of discontent. And this was eating at my health, my marriage and our ministry.

I came to the point where I had to ask Craig's forgiveness for my critical attitude toward him. I confessed my doubts and fears to him, and asked him what to do about my friendship with Clara. We decided to wait until our next fellowship meeting that Thursday evening.

After we were all seated in the living room, Craig opened with prayer and asked the Holy Spirit to guide us into truth. Then we asked Clara if she would like to share with us the discernment she had about the elders and Craig. This was done in a positive way, to give her a chance to speak openly—perhaps she had some points worth hearing. As she began to talk, her usual soft, sweet voice changed—soon she was whining and accusing. It was like watching a beautiful mask being peeled back to reveal her true face underneath. I felt as if God was allowing us to see the real Clara.

Midway through her angry harangue, Clara realized her religious facade had slipped and that we were looking at her with new understanding. She tried to put on a gracious smile and lower her voice, but it was too late. We had seen beneath the surface and she knew it.

That was the last time we ever saw her. I found out later that she joined another church and was eventually elected as an elder. In that position she caused dissention, and a split occurred that destroyed a once-thriving church.

Moreover, I saw how easy it is to control and to be controlled by a religious "front." Both Craig and I are much more cautious these days about the "advice" we receive—and the advice we give.

Fortunately, Elaine came to realize how easily she'd been manipulated because of a trap that was baited with shame— a deep sense of defectiveness. Shame often serves as the conduit for another's control, and women are perhaps more susceptible to this type of manipulation because they are often more interested in relationships than men are. Researchers even think that "there probably is a biological predisposition in females to caretaking behavior."[1]

Most of us feel that we are failing in one or more of our relationships anyway—we may not be the best wife, mother,

---

[1]"Mind," Horizons, *U. S. News & World Report* (August 8, 1988), pp. 54, 55.

daughter or friend that we could be. It's easy to see how this perception can make us easy prey for the control of another person.

Elaine's experience made me look at my own motives for ministry, and I realized that I considered myself to be everyone's "savior." Jesus said, "My yoke is easy and my burden is light" (Matthew 11:30), but because I took on burdens that Jesus did not give me, they became too heavy. I needed to get out from under the false sense of responsibility I had assumed for the lives of other people. For the first time, I found I was able to say *no* to people who wanted me to assume a responsibility that should not be mine. No longer controlled by other people's needs, I was now able to respond to the Spirit of God. I especially noticed a difference in our ministry with inner-city drug addicts. I didn't take it as a personal failure if delivered addicts made the decision to return to drugs. Paul said, "I planted the seed, Apollos watered it, but *God made it grow*" (1 Corinthians 3:6, italics added). God is the only one in control of spiritual growth.

Because I know how I am manipulated by other Christians who perceive which "spiritual" buttons to push, I have become aware of the technique in myself. I ask myself how often I have used guilt, irritability, anger, doubt and fear in order to get people to do what I think is best for them—with the highest spiritual motives, of course!

When I refuse to relax in God's plan and timing, but turn to my own manipulations—with children, husband, pastor, brother or sister in Christ—I am falling into the ultimate control trap: *I am attempting to take the place of God!* Besides the utter arrogance of such a position, from the outset it is a pointless struggle; God always wins!

Here are several considerations if you find yourself *struggling* spiritually to get something accomplished in the way you see fit:

*"I'm not angry at God!"* It's hard to think that we are in a struggle with *God* over something—that we are in opposition to Him. But it may be true. The old adage, "The buck stops here," is never more true than in our relationship with God. After all, He is the Prime Mover in this universe, the Alpha and Omega—the beginning and the end—and ultimately sovereign. In fact, most anger is misdirected: When we are angry at our parents, husband, boss, kids, pastor, church, politicians

or "the system," we may, in fact, be angry at God. After all, God could change things . . . if He wanted to, we think. William Backus, author of *The Hidden Rift With God*, points out that most people deny their anger at God because "it's too terrible to admit."[2] As a result, they may suffer physical or emotional consequences.

Myrna, for example, suffered daily headaches, and they were getting worse. She knew she was angry at her husband because he would not assume the spiritual headship in their home. "I'm tired of trying to be the spiritual leader with the children," she complained to me.

Myrna viewed herself as a very serious Christian, and the thought that she was angry with God diminished her opinion of herself—so she denied it. But her deep anger toward God led her to take control and attempt to change her husband into the leader she thought he should be. She *knew* how to make him jump through the right hoops, and she set out to do it.

Noted author Philip Yancey writes, "True atheists do not, I presume, feel disappointed in God. They expect nothing and receive nothing. But those who commit their lives to God, no matter what, instinctively expect something in return."[3] Our expectations then set us up for disappointment. All of us, no doubt, have felt at some time that God has forgotten us, cheated us, been unappreciative of our commitment, or neglected to answer our prayers. This translates into anger, which can lead us to take control of the situation. And some of us, unfortunately, have learned how to control using spiritual "techniques."

How do we use our *spirituality* to manipulate others? Let's look again at the three basic roots of control—fear, anger and shame—in this context.

*"We don't want to disappoint God, do we?"* Let's face it—all of us have used guilt at some time to control others. We may be subtle in the way we do it. ("Oh, you aren't going to teach Sunday school this year? Well, I guess we'll just have to drop that class since no one wants to take it.") Or we may be more obvious. ("I know you have applied for work at City Hospital,

[2]William Backus, *The Hidden Rift With God* (Minneapolis, Minn.: Bethany House Publishers, 1990), p. 39.
[3]Philip Yancey, *Disappointment With God* (Grand Rapids, Mich.: Zondervan Publishing House, 1988), p. 37.

but God showed me that you are supposed to donate your time at our church's free clinic downtown.") Underneath lies the glaring fact: This person, or their choice, does not fit into my scheme or perception of how things should be; so I try to use spirituality and responsibility toward God to make the person do what I want.

Cora's husband is an alcoholic. He doesn't join her and their children in church on Sunday because he's sleeping off a binge from the night before. Cora doesn't know that the real reason he avoids church is his deep shame about his drinking problem. Cora's looks of contempt and innuendos about his lack of spirituality only increase his own self-loathing and have convinced him that God couldn't possibly be interested in him.

At church, Cora is quick to share with others her husband's latest escapades and the strain of living with a man who is so obviously in sin. She rarely mentions that in spite of his drinking problem, he still supports his family well, and the lovely home they have is a testimony to his hard work.

She can't be blamed for her determination to ensure that her two boys don't fall into the same habits as their father, but her insistence that they attend church with her and participate in all the youth group activities has an "edge" to it. She frequently points out to them the failures of their father and warns them that if they don't attend church faithfully they will probably end up like him. Her oldest son, Sam, who is fourteen, has already shown signs of rebellion, and she has complained to her pastor about his father's bad influence. She doesn't believe in divorce for a Christian, but wonders if the boys would benefit by a separation.

Because Cora's husband is an alcoholic and also an unbeliever, it is easy for Cora to fall into the trap of trying to change his behavior through guilt-producing remarks. But even Christian husbands are sometimes treated like this. Amazingly, the number-one complaint wives have about their *Christian* husbands is that they are not spiritual enough. These wives use the guilt game to prod their husbands into what they perceive as spirituality.

Some of us may be chagrined at hearing ourselves say things like:

- I left your Bible on the kitchen table next to your coffee.

Do you realize you haven't had morning devotions all week?

- I think the reason we're having financial difficulties is because we don't tithe consistently.
- I believe Jamie's rebellion is directly related to our failure to pray together.
- Isn't Jack Brown a spiritual man? Do you know he goes witnessing door-to-door every Saturday morning?

Many of us seem to equate spiritual leadership with the amount of time spent reading the Bible, praying, witnessing, or memorizing scripture verses. We overlook the fact that inward strength of character and fulfilling God-ordained responsibilities make a man a spiritual leader.

One area in which wives consistently fail to recognize and appreciate their husbands is in their commitment to provide for the family. Cora's husband, though an alcoholic, still worked daily to provide for his family. Cora did not see this as a "spiritual" function, and therefore lacked in gratefulness and admiration for her husband in this area. Many wives take for granted that their husband will function as provider, and do not express thankfulness for their work. The role of provider is so important to the spirituality of a man that Paul wrote: "If anyone does not provide for his relatives, and especially for his immediate family, he has denied the faith and is worse than an unbeliever" (1 Timothy 5:8, NIV).

When it comes to spiritual leadership, most men feel unqualified. Their wives may be better at studying the Bible and memorizing verses than they are. Therefore, they're reluctant to initiate spiritual activity in the home, such as evening devotions or prayer before dinner. The wife who nags or manipulates through guilt will discourage her husband and convince him that he never can be a leader.

Guilt-placing *never* helps anyone to change their behavior permanently. A man may appear to change, but it may be just to get you "off his back." The only true change comes from an inward conviction of the Holy Spirit, and He cannot bring conviction while you and I are passing out generous portions of shame and blame. God's power is released through our love and acceptance of each other. I often have to readjust my sights, praying that God will show me the positive qualities in a person so I can focus on those rather than on real or imagined faults. Philippians 4:8 tells us: "Fix your thoughts on what is true and good and right. Think about things that are pure and lovely, and dwell on the fine, *good things in others*" (TLB, italics added).

A friend came to me recently with great concern for her thirteen-year-old son. She knew he was experimenting with smoking and drinking, and his rebellion was affecting his grades in school. She had responded to the crisis by insisting he go to all the youth group activities and that he spend time every morning in daily devotions. She told me that these decrees had only served to fuel his rebellion. Then she said, "I feel that Tony has an evil side to his personality—and I keep warning him that he's just a rebel."

It was plain to see how the pronouncement she made of her son could turn out to be a self-fulfilling prophecy. I told her to think of his positive qualities and begin to focus on those. One very good quality, in fact, is Tony's adventuresome spirit, which was presently being channeled in the wrong direction.

With this advice, she decided not to make an issue of the rebellious attitude he had adopted. She also stopped insisting he attend every youth group activity. Instead, she prayed that God would help her to stay focused on his good qualities and to thank God for them. As she did that, her attitude began to change, and her approach to Tony became one of encouragement and love rather than manipulation through guilt.

Two months later Tony prayed at church, asking Jesus to become Lord of his life—without any prompting from his mom. It was a decision initiated by the Holy Spirit. Not all of us will experience so dramatic and so sudden a change in someone we've prayed for. But this incident illustrates how we can alienate someone from the Lord through pressure tactics, and regain his confidence through affirmation of his good qualities.

Most of us carry around enough shame—we know our failures. Dumping more guilt on a person will push that one toward complete discouragement or rebellion, but it will never accomplish a true change in behavior. When we love, accept and encourage another, we provide the fertile soil for God's Holy Spirit to work and bring conviction.

*"You're going to miss God's best."* When a woman operates from fear, she may use spiritual means to project her fear and

doubt onto others. She may even be so sure she knows God's will for someone that she does not accept the fact that God can speak to him without her help. She becomes adept at planting little seeds of doubt in the minds of those she tries to control:

- Are you sure that house is right for you? Doesn't it seem a little luxurious for someone who's walking with God?
- Jim seems like a nice Christian boy, Mary, but marriage is a lifetime commitment. What about Ed? He said he felt God told him you two were supposed to marry.
- Don't you think Pastor Jim's preaching has been kind of bland lately? He seems to have lost his zeal.
- I know that you like our old church, dear, but God showed me that we wouldn't be able to grow there.
- I can't believe you're going to major in pre-law in college, Dave. When you were born, I dedicated you to God's service as a missionary so your life would have meaning.

Watchman Nee said that Jesus taught us to pray to our Father in heaven, warning that too often we direct our prayers toward the person for whom we are praying. Though his teaching on this subject is somewhat controversial, the following is worth noting:

> Instead of directing your prayer toward God, you concentrate on your thought, your expectation, and your wish and send them out to your friend as a force. Your prayer is like a bow which shoots your thought, desire and wish as arrows toward your friend. He will be so oppressed by this force that he will do exactly what you have asked for. You may think your prayer is answered. But let me tell you, it is not God who answers your prayer, for you have not prayed to Him.[4]

Whether or not prayer has its own "force," nonetheless the Bible tells us that our tongue has the power to bless or curse. "We praise the Lord and Father with it; with it we also *curse* men who have been made in the likeness of God. From the same mouth blessing and *cursing* proceed. This is not right, my brothers, it must not be this way" (James 3:9–10, italics added).

Also, the New Testament in Galatians 5:20 warns believers

---

[4]Watchman Nee, *The Latent Power of the Soul* (New York: Christian Fellowship Publishers, Inc., 1972), pp. 46, 47.

against falling into the sin of witchcraft, one of the works of the flesh. Witchcraft is basically trying to get someone else to do your will. The thought that our "well-meaning" prayers for others might actually border on the sphere of witchcraft is frightening. We need to exercise extreme caution when we presume to tell another person—whether husband, child, parents, friends or pastor—what God's will is for them. Oswald Chambers wrote that we can lead a man to Christ, but only Christ can lead him on from there.

Quite often a pastor will be plagued by a strong group of controlling people within the church—either men or women. They will usually be the ones who run the ministries and have the ear of the others. They may use their influence to plant little doubts and fears about the ability of the pastor, criticize his wife and children, or gossip about him. Eventually, when the pastor finds out and confronts them, they can say: "Well, *everybody* else agrees with me."

John and I once fellowshipped with a church that was destroyed in just that way—in this case, by a few controlling women who sowed doubt and fear. The church went from 200 to about 30 people, and eventually they too disbanded. Be warned: We put ourselves under God's wrath when we try to control with doubts and fears. Proverbs 6:16–19 says the Lord hates anyone who "stirs up dissension among brothers."

We tread upon holy ground when we presume we know God's plan for another's life. In truth, we don't even know our own future: "In his heart a man plans his course, but the Lord determines his steps" (Proverbs 16:9). We may make our plans, but God is sovereign and He will determine our path. Rather than attempt to manipulate others into our will, we ought to concentrate on encouraging them to seek God for *His* will in their life.

*"I've never seen anything so un-Christian!"* Have you ever run into the kind of person who flashes around "God's anger" and the implied threat of His judgment? This person believes that holiness means a lack of joy and spontaneity, because "Christianity is serious business."

Iona's kids want to wear blue jeans to school because "everybody else does"—but she just finished lecturing them on proper dress for Christian boys and girls: skirts for girls, dress pants for boys. After all, they are "ambassadors for Christ," and they need to look the part.

Long ago, Iona's kids learned to quit asking if they could

get a television set. She has told them repeatedly about the dangers of such worldliness and the corruption of the flesh. Far worse than the actual restriction is her tone of voice and manner, and it may not be long before her kids are convinced that God is a very hard taskmaster indeed, and that perhaps any fun or laughter or joy is only to be found "in the world."

In the parable of the talents (Matthew 25:14–20), the servant who received the one talent failed to use it and incurred the Master's wrath because he said, "I knew that you are a hard man . . . So I was afraid . . ." If parents are harsh, angry, and judgmental, then a child may reason that God must be like his parents. This instills an unhealthy fear in the child that, like the servant in the parable, he can never please God. So why even try?

A friend of mine who has struggled with fear and an extreme people-pleasing mentality was raised by a mother who viewed herself as a "prophet." Elsa remembers numerous occasions when they would be sitting in church and her mother would stand up and denounce the church or the pastor or the elders, then motion to Elsa and the other children to stand up and follow her out of the church. They walked down the aisle with the whole congregation staring at them.

Elsa was bound by a fear that she would displease someone and have to suffer the awful stares of others. She was a Christian, but one who served God out of fear rather than love for Him. Now in her mid-forties, she still has not been able to fully grasp the grace of God, and sometimes wonders if her Christianity is real or whether she is merely bound to religion by fear.

Fifteen years ago, my husband and I attended Bill Gothard's Basic Life Principles Advanced Seminar on the motivational gifts. When he taught on the prophet—the person who sees the world in black-and-white—John turned to me and said, "So that explains your behavior." We laughed about it, because Bill warned the husbands that if they were married to someone with a prophetic disposition they were in for some tough times.

Those insights on motivation changed our lives, though. I could finally see that John's very practical gift of organization (which I never considered "spiritual") was just as spiritual as my strong adherence to God's Word and its principles. And he could see why I was always so concerned about God's reputation, justice, and reckoning with sin. As Gothard teaches, people with a prophetic motivation can be very critical, but that criticism is just the negative side of a gift of discernment. That understanding really liberated me!

I had always hated my critical, judgmental spirit, but now I could see it was the negative side of a spiritual gift that God intended for good. After that, as I prayed about the problems I discerned, I adjusted my requests to asking God for mercy and deliverance rather than judgment.

The greatest turn-around in my attitude, though, began when I started to teach a Bible study at a state drug rehabilitation center ten years ago. I was suddenly face-to-face with inner-city drug addicts, many of whom had served prison terms for everything from robbery to rape; and most of the women had become prostitutes to support their habit. These were people I would have found easy to judge and condemn. But as I got to know them, I realized that they were very hurting people, and what they needed were not pronouncements of judgment but assurance of God's mercy. I began to understand *grace*: "But where sin increased, *grace* increased all the more" (Romans 5:20, NIV, italics added). So, for ten years I have consistently taught the grace and mercy of God— and I have probably benefited the most from those lessons.

Because my motivation is prophetic, I still get angry over injustice and I experience great concern for God's reputation. (I had a very hard time because of this during the recent scandals in Christian leadership.) But I am learning to judge the situation, not the person. There is no question that God wants us to be grieved about issues such as abortion-on-demand, and to do what we can to combat this evil dividing our nation. But we must be careful not to step over the line into judgment of *individuals*. God has said, "Do not take revenge, my friends, but leave room for God's wrath, for it is written: 'It is mine to avenge; I will repay,' says the Lord" (Romans 12:19).

## Deeply Dissatisfied People

In my experience, people who try to control spiritually are not satisfied with *themselves*, and are not satisfied with God. Jonah could not run away from his God-ordained duty to preach repentance to Nineveh, and he knew he could not control God and get Him to destroy the city. As a result, he got angry, depressed, and sank into despair.

How much depression can be traced to anger at God because He won't do what we think should be done? Many Christian women who are distressed about spiritual imperfections in others are really angry at themselves, and angry at God for allowing an imperfect world with imperfect people to go on, seemingly without His interference.

If you recognize that you have a tendency to manipulate others spiritually, you also need to see the grave danger of linking manipulation with spirituality. First, because you are putting yourself in direct opposition to God—a frightening position—where you will always come out the loser. Secondly—and still more frightening—you put yourself in the place of being ultimately deceived.

Queen Jezebel of the Old Testament has long been characterized as the symbol of the ultimate controlling woman. Although you and I may feel that we have nothing in common with this evil woman, a look at her religious control and its disastrous results may be enlightening.

Jezebel had a strong controlling spirit that was joined with religion. She had nearly 1000 prophets of Baal (1 Kings 18:19) who still used the name of Jehovah and prophesied falsely (Jeremiah 23:16–32). Because of this, the ordinary people were bewildered and wavered "between two opinions" (1 Kings 18:21). The combination of her desire to control along with her "spirituality" brought confusion to the people. Similarly, wherever we join our control over another with spirituality, the result will bring confusion.

This queen's dominating personality combined with religion caused the great prophet Elijah to run in fear of her (1 Kings 19:3). From this example, it is easy to see how a pastor might fear a strong woman or group of women who seek to dictate spiritual matters in the church. There is a certain power in operation when we assert our will through the vehicle of spirituality. James says that when we take a dominating, assertive position, "Such 'wisdom' does not come down from heaven but is earthly, unspiritual, of the devil" (James 3:15, NIV). When we attempt to manipulate another person spiritually, we automatically set ourselves in opposition to God. This can open a person up to demonic deception.

Jezebel did not initially set out to do evil. She wanted her way and thought she knew what was best for her husband, King Ahab, and for Israel. It would be a rare person, indeed, who would consciously choose to bring evil upon themselves and their family, but this is the deception that can occur when we take control. Each of us chooses what we *perceive* to be good, but the problem lies in our *perception*. When we presume to know what is best for others, we put ourselves in the place of God in their lives. God can do nothing but stand in opposition to us, for our own good.

Jezebel may be an extreme example of the controlling woman, and perhaps we can relate better to Moses' sister, Miriam. Miriam was a godly woman, a prophetess (Exodus 15:20), and a leader among the women of Israel. It was Miriam who led the women in a dance after the crossing of the Red Sea. She must have had an appealing and strong personality. God used her as long as she was in right relationship with the authority over Israel that He had established. One day, however, she began to use her spiritual position to speak against Moses because she was unhappy with his marriage to a Cushite woman. She may even have been jealous of this woman for "usurping" her First-Lady-of-the-Land position. She wanted to be in control and said, "Hasn't he (God) also spoken through us?" In other words, "God told me too!" (Numbers 12:2).

Miriam tried to use her spirituality to control Moses, and God didn't like it. In fact, God allowed her to become leprous. Miriam had to be isolated from the camp for seven days before God healed her. Leprosy is a striking physical symbol of Miriam's spiritual problem. God wanted to isolate Miriam because her spiritual manipulation would have spread like a disease among the Israelites and caused great disunity and confusion. God does not take lightly those who try to use their spirituality or position to manipulate others. Even though God loved Miriam, and she had been greatly used by Him in the past, He cut her off from her people rather than allow her to "infect" them.

There is another side to this matter, of course. God has placed various gifts within His Body (1 Corinthians 12)—gifts of wisdom, knowledge, and distinguishing between spirits, to name a few. There are times when a person so gifted needs to share what God has revealed to him or her. But how do we know whether we are to tell someone else of an insight or leading from God?

First, and most important, we must be sure this "guidance" is not our own agenda. Nor should it be given in a dictatorial manner. If, for instance, I've been praying for someone and feel that God has given me knowledge or a scripture verse for that person, my approach to them must be: "I think God has given me this scripture for you concerning your situation, but you need to pray and check it out for yourself." In this way, you give the person room to make the final decision before God as to whether your thoughts are from Him or your own imagination. Ultimately, each one of us must stand before God, responsible for our own decisions.

My husband often has people approach him with "guidance" for the church. He encourages those who feel they are prophetic to tell him what God is saying to them. In fact, he believes a church that won't listen to their prophets is a church that will lose its edge. But John also warns that once you share what you believe God is saying, you need to let it go. Now it is up to the Holy Spirit to guide the other person in discerning how to respond to it. This is where many people stumble— they are upset because they don't see the other responding in a way they think he should. Then they begin to talk to others about it or make pronouncements of doom. This type of behavior indicates a spirit of control, rather than submission to the will of God.

Before people can receive our insights, they must respect our walk with God. Congregations cringe when the "church-hopper," the "self-proclaimed prophet," or the "wild-eyed fanatic" stands up to share a testimony or give a prophetic statement. They need to see in us the Spirit of Jesus, who is humble and gentle in His approach (Philippians 2:5–8).

Using spirituality to control others and get our own way is unfair play. It's like the child who claims, "Daddy told me," when his daddy never told him. Or the little girl who shouts at her playmate, "Jesus says we're supposed to share!" when she wants the new toy for herself. It's taking God's place in the life of another to get them to fulfill *our* plan for their life rather than to seek God's will. It is the ultimate control trap and it brings us into the ultimate conflict—opposing God.

The good news is that if we have used spirituality to control, we can always turn back to God and receive His forgiveness. We may have to go to other people whom we have tried to control and ask their forgiveness, too. God is eager to forgive and to correct our course. As with Miriam, He will restore us to health—physically, emotionally, and most important, spiritually.

*To the woman he said, ". . . with pain you will give birth to children. Your desire will be for your husband, and he will rule over you."*

*Genesis 3:16*

# 15

# *Spiritual Roots*

For the majority of this book, we have considered what some psychologists, secular and Christian, have to say on such topics as fear, anger, shame, and relationship dynamics. We've also looked at scriptures that balance and support their discoveries, and we have related stories of Christian women who are learning to recognize and escape from their own control traps.

In this chapter, I want to reverse the process and look at what God himself wants us to know when we step out from under His order. From the Scriptures, we will see what happens when we set out to order the world according to our inner emotional drives or religious-spirited demands, rather than operating in the power of His grace and love.

First, I want to issue a caution. There are two ways in which you could take what is written here and apply it in a wrong way. What we're about to consider is strong medicine from the Word of God. But keep in mind that the Word of God was not meant to be used as a weapon to goad other people. So don't give in to the temptation of thinking of "other women who need to read this." On the other hand, don't give yourself a soul-lashing if any of the words sting your heart. The sting of the Holy Spirit is like healing, preserving salt, meant for cleansing, renewing and freeing.

Finally, it is very important for you to realize as a Christian that when you feel the prick or sting of the Holy Spirit, it is not a threat to your eternal salvation. But it *is* a matter of His calling you into account according to the spiritual law of sowing and reaping (Galatians 6:7). By that I mean, He wants to reveal to us ways that we have been spending our energy on lifeless nonessentials, so that we can let them go and begin to live for things that are eternal (Matthew 6:19–34).

## The Spiritual Root of Control

The root of a problem is always at the beginning. In the garden, after the Fall, God pronounced a curse on the serpent, the man, and the woman. In all three instances, the curse struck at the very root of the ego, the "personhood" of each.

The serpent was "more crafty than any of the wild animals the Lord God had made" (Genesis 3:1). The word "crafty" denotes pride and cunning and comes from a root word that means smooth in a negative sense. Because of the serpent's sin against mankind, God caused this proud, cunning animal to spend the rest of his days crawling on his belly, eating the dust of the earth.

A man's ego and self-image are tied up in his ability to provide for his family. Most men see their job as an extension of themselves. God cursed this ability: Though the man would sweat and strain to provide for his family, many days his work would only yield "thorns and thistles" (Genesis 3:18).

Women gain the greatest ego satisfaction from their family—husband and children. Yet children are brought forth in pain. I believe an extension of that curse is the pain a mother feels later in life when she sees one of her children in rebellion. Proverbs 10:1 says, "A wise son brings joy to his father, but a foolish son brings grief to his mother." The pain of the son's rebellion could be an echo of the curse.

Most importantly, I want to focus here on the second part of the curse on the woman, an indication of the power conflict that can exist between husband and wife. God said, "Your desire will be for your husband, and he will rule over you." The word desire is from the Hebrew word *tshuwqah*, meaning stretching out after. The root of the word means to run after or to run over. The literal translation of Genesis 3:16 may very well be: "Your desire will be [to control] your husband and he will [desire to dominate] you."

Before the Fall, God created the woman to be a *helper* to

the man (Genesis 2:18). Therefore, the husband's leadership was established even before the Fall and the woman's submission is inherent in the term *helper*. Many women react to this term, but the Holy Spirit is also called "the Helper" (John 14:15, KJV). Apparently He does not feel it is degrading or shameful to be called a Helper. We women should consider it an honor to be referred to by the same term as the third Person of the Trinity.

The Fall corrupted Eve's *willing* submission, and because of the continuing effects of the curse a woman still battles two opposing desires: the desire to have her husband take the lead, and the desire to control and lead herself. Men also have to fight the inclination to rule by domination rather than by loving leadership. For this reason the command to the wife in the New Testament is to "submit" (Ephesians 5:25; 1 Peter 3:7), and the command to her husband is to love her "as Christ loves the church." (He no doubt has the more difficult challenge!) Now both men and women have to do in obedience to God's command what was once a natural response.

The good news is that "Christ redeemed us from the curse of the law by becoming a curse for us" (Galatians 3:13). With the curse broken, we *can* have the victory over our desire to control, and we can expect to find our greatest source of blessing within the family structure *as we learn to walk in godly submission*, rather than seeking to control through manipulation or domination.

Though our natural root through Eve gives us the tendency toward control and manipulation, John the Baptist preached that Jesus would put an axe to the root of that tree (Luke 3:9). The woman who will walk in freedom and trust is the one who has surrendered to the rule of Jesus in her life. Once the spiritual root of control that connects us to our fleshly nature is severed, we are able to learn a new way of relating to others and to God.

Once we have recognized the sin of control, repented and surrendered this area of our lives to Jesus, we may feel the battle has been won, and the *urge* to control is miraculously erased. Don't be discouraged when you again feel this desire (because you will!); you *don't have to give in* to it. The Holy Spirit will help you resist this temptation to manage and manipulate people and events toward your own plans. And every time you overcome this urge, the old habits of thinking and responding loosen their hold on you. There will come a time when control will no longer be a major issue in your life. This is what Romans 12:2 refers to as "the renewing of your mind."

## Antagonism Toward Men

This is another hard area to address, but we cannot ignore it. Many women want to dominate in their relationships with men because of an underlying distrust, even hatred, of the male sex. In my experience, a very high majority—perhaps 90 percent—of the women I have counseled have some measure of hatred toward men that propels them to stay in control. This hatred may have its beginnings with a father who was either physically or emotionally absent. Pierre Mornell, author of *Passive Men, Wild Women*, says, "Regardless of the reason—dead, divorced, indifferent, outsider or simply working too many hours a day—most of my generation, I think, suffered from this absent-father syndrome."[1]

What little girl does not want a strong, protecting father-figure to shield her from hurt and disappointment? If her father is not there for her she feels abandoned, and eventually that abandonment can turn into hatred (even if repressed) toward him for disappointing her. If she has been physically, sexually, or verbally abused by a man, especially if by her father, that anger is likely to be turned outward toward men in general. When this woman marries—who has been disappointed in this way during childhood, and who carries hatred toward men as a result—she has romanticized expectations that her husband will make up to her for all the failures of her father. In fact, the more unhappy the relationship with her own father, the greater the expectation that the "right" man will make her happy. It is easy to see how these expectations doom a marriage relationship to fail, and how a woman becomes further entrenched in her hatred of men.

Ruth's grandmother was married to a physically abusive man, and she often advised Ruth not to marry. During her high school years, Ruth's parents divorced and her father remarried a woman with two teenage daughters. Ruth felt abandoned by her dad, and the pain was further intensified because

---

[1]Pierre Mornell, *Passive Men, Wild Women* (New York: Ballantine Books, 1980), p. 42.

he now had two other daughters to look after. Ruth didn't marry until she was thirty-two, but she was determined to have a successful marriage. As often happens when a woman carries hatred toward men, according to many counsellors, Ruth married a man who was angry at women. Mike was adopted and felt his natural mother had abandoned him. He took out his anger against his natural mom by treating Ruth in a disrespectful and demeaning manner. Ruth tried to maintain the "peace" in their home by allowing her husband to treat her unkindly in this manner without resisting it or confronting him with it.

After ten years of marriage, they were on the brink of a separation. Instead, they decided to go to marriage counseling. Ruth learned to forgive her father and deal with her hatred of men, and Mike learned to forgive his mother and give up his hatred of women. Both had to learn new ways of relating to each other. Once Ruth was released of her hatred of men, she no longer felt she had to be punished by men and no longer gave in to Mike's verbal abuse. Mike began to have a new respect for Ruth and to treat her in a more loving manner.

Had it not been for the fact that Ruth and Mike were Christians, they probably would not have worked so hard to save their marriage. They most likely would have divorced, and Ruth would have proved that her grandmother was right and that she was justified in her hatred of men. This is how a man-hating spirit can pass from generation to generation, until the power of Christ is allowed to break the chain reaction.

A mother who has this antagonism toward men will likely raise a son with a poorly defined masculinity. She may love her son, but her underlying hatred of men will subconsciously destroy or redefine what is masculine in him. Sometimes this is done, oddly enough, by bonding closely with her son, being his best friend, and keeping him from having a relationship with his father, thus robbing him of the opportunity for his masculinity to develop. She may destroy her son's initiative and aggressiveness, two strong masculine traits, and produce instead a passive, ineffectual, even effeminate male. If she is open in her disapproval of men, she likely will raise a son who disapproves of women, even hates them.

Ghetto cultures are largely matriarchal societies. The ghetto woman typically hates men, often because of abuse by the men in her past, and the men are generally marked by their singular lack of initiative.

The story of King David and his wife, Michal, the daughter of Saul, reveals God's view of women despising men. As Michal watched King David leaping and dancing as the ark of the Lord returned to the city, "she *despised* him in her heart" (2 Samuel 6:16).

We too may despise certain men in our own lives. You may "hate" the way your husband makes that nervous gesture just before he says grace; you find your father's eating habits disgusting; you can't stand the way your pastor drags out a story and then ruins the punchline; you are embarrassed by your son's lack of athletic ability at the little league game. We may never say anything outwardly, the way Michal eventually did to David, but this type of perspective can translate from specific men to males in general.

The last mention of Michal in the Scripture comes after that incident: "And Michal . . . had no children to the day of her death" (2 Samuel 6:23). Her despising attitude easily could be transferred to her children, and God did not want to infect the line of David that would produce the future Messiah.

Once hatred of men becomes firmly entrenched in a society, deep trouble will follow. There will be an explosion of homosexuality, and men who are unwilling to make a commitment to a woman. Both problems stem from the same root—mothers who hate men. As men take the more passive role, women rise to the top in leadership, and God's order is inverted. God's warning to Israel, which follows, is just as relevant today.

## Women in Authority

> As for my people, children are their oppressors, and *women rule over them*. O my people, they which lead thee cause thee to err, and destroy the way of thy paths. (Isaiah 3:12, KJV, italics added)

Since World War II, when large numbers of women first began working outside the home in factories because of the shortage of men, women have moved into all areas of leadership. Women now manage a good number of our nation's financial institutes; increasing numbers of homes in this country have no father-figure, and a child's thinking is largely formed by the mother; when the child enters school, it is primarily women who will teach and train him, and very possibly, when he enters the work force his supervisor will be a woman. Women now make up 44.3 percent of the work force. Sunday worship services are 60–62 percent female, and women are now bishops, pastors, elders and priests.

I am not saying that women don't make very capable leaders, or should never be in those kinds of positions, but we need to be aware of some snares and guidelines for women in leadership. We know that God used a woman—Deborah—to lead the whole nation of Israel at one perilous time in their history (Judges 4 & 5), but as far as I can tell it was the exception, not the rule.

The most obvious pitfall is that a married woman in a leadership position might have a hard time making the switch to being a wife in submission to her husband when she comes home, especially if she is used to giving directions to men during the day. At work she makes the final decisions, so it could be difficult for her to submit to her husband, especially if he is by nature slower in his decision-making process. This wife will need to make some mental and emotional "switches" when she walks in the door of her home.

A second point is that a woman may possess skills and even natural talent that make it hard for her to submit to someone else in those particular areas. A wife who is a financial consultant at the local bank may have a hard time submitting to her husband's decisions in the area of household finances. A woman may be the top salesperson in a firm and a whiz at making motivational speeches. So on Sundays, when she listens to her pastor in church, she may be mentally evaluating his sermon and secretly despising his lack-luster style. A college-educated daughter may feel that her dad, who only finished high school, is unable to give her any advice.

Scripture says the "head of every man is Christ, and the head of the woman is man . . ." (1 Corinthians 11:3). Notice it says "man" and "woman," not husband and wife, indicating that God's plan for orderly authority extends beyond the marriage relationship and includes single as well as married women. Something can happen to women in leadership that makes difficulties in submitting to men—whether husband, father, elder, or pastor. A woman who is used to "calling the shots" could feel: "Why should I listen to him? I make more money, know more, have more responsibility at work, etc."

Another factor that we will discuss in the next section is the stress involved in leadership. Our large city had a woman mayor for one term, and it was amazing to see the stress of the office played out in her face. Even though she had a face-lift mid-way through her four-year term, she aged dramatically during that time. Her manner also became much more abrasive, especially toward those who criticized her. There no doubt are many women mayors who do very well and handle the position with grace and dignity. But I believe that any woman in leadership, whether in the church or in business, needs the safe-guard of a protective and trusted male figure. It may be her immediate superior at work, a father, husband, pastor, or close friend, but she should have someone to go to for counsel and to talk over her frustrations and questions.

As women become more and more visible in positions traditionally held by men, men can become more and more passive. Dr. Pierre Mornell blames the problem of male passivity and domineering women on the pressures of modern life. But it is an age-old problem—one that first appeared in the garden when Eve usurped Adam's decision-making authority.

God's order is clear in 1 Corinthians 11:3, and when that order is disrupted, the family will become out of balance, and even open to demonic influence. I am not talking here about the single mother whose husband is no longer around, or the married woman whose husband has all but abandoned her and her children or has chosen to withdraw from his role as husband and father. A woman in these circumstances can readily count on God's loving protection, His presence with her and her children.

But we cannot ignore God's order and lightly violate it. Orderliness governs all of creation. As He laid the earth's foundations, marked off its dimensions and set the footings, the angels shouted for joy (Job 38:4–7), for the world was previously in chaos (Genesis 1:2). Science is built on the knowledge that there are unchangeable laws governing the universe. The authority structure of the world is established by God (Romans 13), and in His churches God has an established order also (1 Corinthians 14:40).

Nature presents an interesting analogy here. Since the original orderliness of God's creation was upset by sin, people have continued to disturb God's orderly universe in one way or another. When God designed our earth, He provided exactly the right atmosphere to sustain plant and animal life. The fluorocarbons in cleaning products, deodorants, hairsprays and perfumes are slowly eating away the protective ozone layer that protects us from excess radiation. The long-term effects of this radiation will adversely affect plant, animal and human life. The climate changes we are beginning to experience relate to the disappearance of this protective layer.

In a similar way, God has also established a "protective layer" around the family unit. But when God's order begins to break down—when fathers abdicate their role of headship, when women begin to rule, and children stop obeying their parents—then there is a corresponding breakdown in the protective layer.

This protective layer is called a "wall" or a "hedge" in Scripture. Satan accused God of protecting Job and his household with a hedge of protection (Job 1:10). Because of that protective covering, Satan could not touch him. In this case God allowed Satan to breach this hedge to allow Job to be tested. This was not due to any sin on Job's part. But in other instances the hedge can be breached as a result of sin.

God not only puts a hedge around an individual, but He can also put a hedge around a nation. God maintained this protective circle around the nation of Israel, but their failure to walk in righteousness led to God's judgment. He describes in Scripture how He would administer that judgment: "I will take away [Israel's] hedge, and it will be destroyed; I will break down its wall, and it will be trampled" (Isaiah 5:5). We are experiencing something similar to this in our culture today. Because of sin and unrighteousness, the hedge that once kept the U.S. a strong nation is fast disappearing. We are bankrupt spiritually, and we see demon-influenced forces overtaking our nation.

Through the prophet Ezekiel, God also warned Israel that they had not repaired the breaks in the wall around them, that it would not "stand firm in the battle on the day of the Lord" (Ezekiel 13:5). That God is talking about a spiritual rather than a physical wall is evident later in the chapter. God accuses the prophets of speaking, " 'Peace,' when there is no peace, and because, when a flimsy wall is built, they cover it with whitewash." Something like this is happening today.

God's great promises are glibly recited without mention of the conditions necessary for the fulfillment of the promises. People are assured of God's love and blessing without the warning to repent.

God offers us a wall of protection from the onslaught of satanic activity, a place of refuge and safety in God's order. Our country, our government, our cities, our churches, and our families are in crises. God's established order provides covering and protection. When we pervert or try to reinterpret God's order, we suffer the consequences: "And whoso breaketh a hedge, a serpent shall bite him" (Ecclesiastes 10:8).

Our hedges have been broken down and the Serpent has sunk his teeth into many of our families. The result of that demonic influence is seen in the unprecedented rise of child abuse, run-away children, homosexuality, divorce, teen suicide and pregnancies, abortion, and drug addiction. All these problems relate back to disturbances within the family structure. The floodgates are opened for the evil tide that threatens to undermine every family foundation in America today. Men will have to answer to God for abdicating their role as head, but women will also have to answer for their part in the undermining of that headship.

## God's Judgment

In the book of Isaiah, after God charges the women with ruling, He warns of a coming judgment, beginning with the "elders and leaders of the people" (Isaiah 3:14). It is understandable that God judges the leaders first, because Scripture warns that they will have to give an account for those under their care (Hebrews 13:17) and that teachers will be judged more severely (James 3:1). In fact, no one can deny that God is already at work judging those who are in leadership. But I was surprised to see that after He judges the leaders, the very next group that God judges are the women!

> The Lord says, "The women of Zion are haughty, walking along with outstretched necks, flirting with their eyes, tripping along with mincing steps, with ornaments jingling on their ankles. . . . In that day the Lord will snatch away their finery: the bangles and headbands and crescent necklaces, the earrings and bracelets and veils, the headdresses and ankle chains and sashes, the perfume bottles

and charms, the signet rings and nose rings, the fine robes and the capes and cloaks, the purses and mirrors, and the linen garments and tiaras and shawls. Instead of fragrance there will be a stench; *instead of well-dressed hair, baldness;* instead of fine clothing, sackcloth; instead of beauty, branding. *Your men will fall by the sword,* your warriors in battle. (Isaiah 3:16–25, italics added).

This rather uncomfortable passage is a word picture from the pen of Isaiah depicting these women as not only proud and seductive but materialistic. The passage includes a list of every cosmetic device used in that day; their one great concern was personal adornment. The sheer magnitude of the catalog of beauty aids should have been enough to convict these women of misplaced dependence.

In like manner, women today can easily direct the desire to be attractive to the externals that are even more readily available today, rather than focusing on the "unfading beauty of a gentle and quiet spirit" (1 Peter 3:4).

Even Christian women can fall prey to the spirit of the world depicted on our TV screens and in beauty magazines. Who has not wished she could afford liposuction or a facelift? A friend told me recently she was actually considering a face-lift until the plastic surgeon told her it would cost $10,000. "At that moment," she said, "I realized I could never justify $10,000 for beauty when millions go to bed hungry each night."

In spite of our preoccupation with fashion and beauty, deep down we really know what is most important. For the last several years, Mother Theresa of Calcutta has been voted the number-one most-admired woman in the annual *Redbook* magazine poll. Isn't it unusual that so many American women admire that old, work-lined, stooped little woman? Yet not many are modeling themselves after her.

## Women and Stress

The women of Isaiah's time also were concerned mainly with outward appearance, so God said He would take away all the things they depended on for their beauty and He struck them with a disease that caused baldness. This was no arbi-trary punishment; hair has a very symbolic meaning in Scrip-ture.

First of all, hair is a symbol of being under authority (1 Corinthians 11:10), and the Scripture says it is given to us as a covering or protection (v. 15). Since these women had usurped authority, they had no covering or protection. God physically demonstrated their spiritual condition by removing the symbol of their covering—their hair.

Secondly, hair is also a woman's glory (1 Corinthians 11:15) when she is fulfilling her role as a helper to a man. Since these women were not fulfilling their assigned role, they were no longer bringing glory to the man and, through the man, to all of the human race (v. 7).

God also sent a disease that would disfigure them and make them an abomination to their former lovers. The stench of this disease would obliterate the beautiful smell of the perfume they wore. We do not know what this particular disease was, but we do know that today women are fast approaching the male statistics for diseases once thought primarily "male diseases."

In an interview with Dr. Hans Selye, pioneer in the field of stress, he stated: "The more the women's movement permits women to take what have usually been considered male jobs, the more women are subject to so-called male diseases—often related to stress—such as cardiac infractions, gastric ulcers and hypertension."[2] When a woman works outside her home and faces the stresses of the business world, any attempts to "manage" her husband and children's lives will compound her personal stress. Home and family should be a place of peace and restoration—for her as well as her husband and children. This movement back and forth between two different worlds requires of her an amazing balancing act.

We also know that cancer is a disease rampant among women today and one particularly related to the attitude of the person. A study which compared women who developed breast cancer with those who had benign breast lumps found that "the central difference between them was the frequency of 'suppression of anger' among those women who were found to have malignancies."[3] Breast cancer is now the third leading cause of death among women; there are about 130,000 new

---

[2]"To Beat Stress—'Learn How to Live,' " *U. S. News & World Report* (March 21, 1977).
[3]Henry Dreher, "Do You Have a Type-C (Cancer Prone) Personality?", *Redbook* (May, 1988), pp. 108, 109, 158.

cases diagnosed each year and that figure is on the increase.[4]

Dr. Susan Jeffers found that in her own case the connection between attitude and cancer was more fact than fiction. In her book *Opening Our Hearts to Men*, she talks about her anger toward men after her divorce: "Yes, I was angry, but so what. They deserved it, and who needed them anyway! I delighted in my newly found female camaraderie. 'If only I could find a man who was just like my girlfriends' was a common lament. We were united in our anger toward men who were almost obsessively our main topic of conversation."[5]

Some time later she was diagnosed with breast cancer and she realized that there were some things she had to change if she was going to survive. She said it was easy to change her diet but found something else much more challenging. "That of course, was *letting go of my anger*. What made the challenge so great was that the basic requirement of getting rid of my anger was to take a brutally honest look at myself instead of pointing my finger at men."[6]

As I mentioned earlier in this chapter, women who are in control—whether of family, home or office—are often those women who have a despising spirit toward men. Besides the added stress of being in a leadership position, they may also have the internal stress of anger. That combination of internal and external stress may tip the balance from the healthy to the disease state. And today that disease is often cancer.

I do not mean to indicate that every woman who has cancer despises men and is controlling or that a woman free from the disease is therefore not angry and controlling. Basic personality enters into the disease equation and some women can handle stress better than others. In fact, sensitive women like Dr. Jeffers may actually be more fortunate. She was able to see the "fruit" of her anger with its resultant control and realize her need to change. Other women may not "eat the fruit of their ways" until much later in life when they see the negative effects on their relationships or children.

The third chapter of Isaiah ends with this sad judgment: "Your men will fall by the sword" (v. 25). Since the women were controlling the nation anyway, God physically took the men away from them. I mentioned earlier in the chapter that many fathers are either physically or emotionally absent from the homes in this nation.

In a recent article called "Locking Dad Out," the author states that up to 80 percent of non-custodial parents have problems getting to see their child or children.[7] The non-custodial parent is usually the father and he—sometimes understandably so—is literally being "locked out."

The passive male of today is a reemergence of an old problem. The men of Isaiah's time also were passive—so passive they let women move into leadership. Today's passive male has special peculiarities: If he is single, he won't commit to marriage; if he is separated from his wife and children, he often refuses to pay child support; if he stays in the marriage, he will often withdraw behind his newspaper, sports or his job. He is occasionally impotent—emotionally or physically. A recent article by a leading feminist was entitled, "What's Happened to All the Men?" Isaiah, chapter 3 might answer her question.

## The Promise of Restoration

A promise of restoration always follows judgment. Because we are God's children, He does not judge us to destroy us but rather to set us on the right path. Accomplishing His purpose includes His restoration and blessing. Isaiah tells the women of his day that they will begin to understand that they have been in rebellion against God:

> In that day seven women will take hold of one man and say, "We will eat our own food and provide our own clothes; only *let us be called by your name*, take away our disgrace! (Isaiah 4:1, italics added).

These women had come full circle. They wanted to rule, to be in charge of their own lives, to control and dominate. Maybe, like many women today, they felt like second-class citizens. But now they are seeing the havoc that has occurred because their role was out of balance. At one time they were in charge—now they are willing to share one man among

---

[7]Barbara Sullivan, "Locking Dad Out," *Chicago Tribune*, Section 7, Style, (Wednesday, February 1, 1989), pp.11–12.

seven women, if only they can have his name.

Today, I believe, we are seeing a similar reversal in thinking among women. During the era of women's liberation, many of the spokespeople, like Germaine Greer, were urging women not to marry but to remain independent. Recent interviews and articles indicate a change from the 70's and 80's drive for independence. A number of recent books by secular women psychologists reflect a dramatic shift in thinking. There is a resurgence of interest in homemaking skills; the single career woman is suddenly aware that her "biological clock is ticking"; women are discovering that the "sensitive" male can be a too-passive male and not at all what they really wanted; and the divorced woman is finding out that life alone does not include the positive aspects she had planned.

There is a similar change among Christian women. Some of us endured the heavy, off-balance "submission" teaching of the 70's that often encouraged manipulation rather than biblical submission. Then we became aware of our own gifts and ministries in the Body of Christ and even moved into some spheres of leadership. Women can have great freedom in the Body of Christ to exercise their gifts and ministries but *under* the authority of the pastor, elders, and, if she is married, her husband. The only area closed to women in the Church is that of government (1 Timothy 3:1–7; Titus 1:6–9). Now it is time for restoration of God's order.

> Then the Lord will create over all of Mount Zion and over those who assemble there a cloud of smoke by day and a glow of flaming fire by night; over all the glory will be a *canopy*. It will be a shelter and shade from the heat of the day, and a refuge and hiding place from the storm and rain. (Isaiah 4:5–6, italics added)

God's imagery of a canopy is another way of looking at His promise to place a spiritual "hedge" around the family. Inherent in this scripture is God's promise of a future Messiah for Israel and a future kingdom, but it can also depict the hedge for families that exists when God's divine order is once again functioning in our personal lives. It is only after we wives submit to the headship of our husbands that God establishes a covering over us, providing an invincible shield against the demonic hosts seeking to destroy the family unit.

"When the enemy shall come like a flood, the Spirit of the

Lord shall lift up a standard against him" (Isaiah 59:19, KJV). Today we are facing a flood of evil: pornography, drugs, Satanism, abortion, child-abuse, incest, and homosexuality. God wants to raise the Church up as His standard. And He will do so when His protection and order are restored in our homes.

## The Good News

As stated at the beginning of this chapter, we have some serious issues to consider as women of God in these difficult times. Fortunately, the fate of the world does *not* rest on our shoulders. We have been given the Holy Spirit, not only to reveal our heart motives, but to walk beside us as Counselor and Helper on our way out of the power of sin in our lives. He is always the bringer of the Good News.

And there is Good News! God *always* provides a way out— or in this case, a way *back* to His full blessing, which He means for you and me to enjoy no matter how far we've strayed from His plan.

The following chapter is an invitation—for God always welcomes us back as His friends (Colossians 1:21–23). And I invite you now to follow His way out of every control trap.

*Then you will know the truth, and the truth will set you free.*

*John 8:32*

# 16

# The Way Out

Paul seemed to feel that remaining single rather than married was best for a Christian so as not to be caught in the trap of trying to please a spouse (1 Corinthians 7:8). He may also have seen that the important roles of wife and mother can easily be distorted by control. How women use their influence in these roles seriously affects their success. Augustus Napier, Ph.D., director of the Family Workshop in Atlanta, found that the most unhappy marriages are those "in which the wife is dominant and 'superfunctional' and the husband is dependent and 'underfunctional.' "[1] Psychologists have also found that the mothers of happy, healthy children had one thing in common—they were serene, relaxed and happy women. "It doesn't seem to matter if a mother is permissive or strict, rich or poor, in the work force or a homemaker. What does matter to the children is the mother's own inner tranquility."[2]

It's hard to be "serene and relaxed" when you're trying to control all the details, large and small, of your family's lives. It's as hard for a man to love a wife who is perpetually uptight and domineering as it is for a woman to love a husband who is distant or unresponsive. And for any woman, married or single, it's difficult to live a joyful, fulfilled life when you feel *you* have to be in control of relationships or situations.

---

[1]Lesley Formen, "The Most Dangerous Relationships a Woman Can Have," *Ladies Home Journal* (September 1990), pp. 106, 112, 114, 115.
[2]"What Makes a Good Mother?," *Good Housekeeping* (August 1986), p. 97.

Hopefully, by this time you've been able to discover the hows and whys of control in your own life. Yes, nearly all of us do it in some measure. This recognition is the beginning of freedom. But understanding is not enough. We must then be willing to turn away from control and its bondage in our lives and the lives of others. To control another's life is to ultimately put oneself in the place of God. It also can rob the life of another, limit it, keep that one from walking in the fullness of God's plan. Eventually, control eats at our own health—emotionally, physically, spiritually.

## Repent

The dictionary definition of repent means "to feel such sorrow for sin or fault as to be disposed to *change one's life. . . .*"[3] When John the Baptist came preaching repentance the crowd asked, "What should we *do* then?" (Luke 3:10, italics added). Insight concerning a problem or sin must be followed by a change in behavior. Instead of remaining in the control mode we need to "change our lives." This means we must trust that God really is in control of the universe and really does want the best for us. To let down our guard and relax allows us to love those close to us without feeling we have to control them. It is difficult for all of us security-minded, controlling women to learn a new approach to life. Difficult—but not impossible.

One of the first steps out of the control mode is to learn to embrace change.

## Change

Let's face it—for most of us, change is a threat. We fear change because we feel we won't be able to adapt. Even a slight deviation from the familiar can bring on a feeling of terrible panic. Control seems necessary for survival.

When a woman senses that her world is slipping out of her control, she responds by fighting for an ever-tighter grip on all that spells familiarity, security. Of course, she will eventually meet resistance—and then she may hold on even tighter.

---

[3]*The Random House Dictionary of the English Language* (New York: Random House, 1971), p. 1216.

The only way out of that endless spiral is to accept change and release her grip.

I sensed I was losing control of the nice little world I'd built for my family the night before our firstborn, John, was ready to leave for college. I couldn't sleep, and as I lay quietly in bed so I wouldn't wake my husband, I had the strangest sensation: I felt like little parts of my self were breaking off and drifting away. I asked God what I was feeling. The thought came a few minutes later that this is what it feels like to lose control. It was the beginning of a period of radical change in our home. The next year our second child, Shannon, would leave for college, and the next year, Tom, our third child. A line from an old rhyme ran through my mind: "Ladybug, ladybug, fly away home, your house is on fire, your children all gone." I wanted to curl up in the middle of our home and pull our life back together—the way it had always been.

As I continued to pray, God seemed to say through my thoughts that I could either relax and let it happen or I could try to hold on and make myself and everyone else miserable. That night I made an important decision: I decided to relax and embrace the changes that inevitably would come into my life.

That was eleven years ago and I have been through many changes since that time—and every time I am tempted to resist the change, I remember my decision and instead "lean into" the new challenge.

Most of us tend to view all change as negative. In fact, a few years ago some psychologists found they could correlate the amount of stress a person was under by the number of changes in his or her life. They assigned scores for each life change, and by adding the scores, they came up with an individual's stress index.

Even some of our descriptions of change indicate a negative rather than positive outlook. The physiological change that marks our transition from a girl to a woman is sometimes called "the curse"; marriage is called "the ball and chain"; the birth of a child is referred to as being "tied down," and then when the children leave home we face an "empty nest." I was so worried about dealing with the "empty-nest syndrome" that it took me a while to realize what a wonderful period of life it could be. I finally would have the time to do some of the things I'd put off for years, and my husband and

I loved the freedom of finally being a *couple* again!

If we see change only as negative and stressful, then naturally we are going to resist it. But if we recognize the need to embrace change and don't prejudice a situation, we may be surprised by what God will do.

Eileen lost her job when the firm she worked for moved. At first she was frantic, because her salary went to pay college tuitions. Then she decided to use her time to market the boutique earrings she made as a hobby. Now she has a thriving business that she runs from her home, and she also earns *more* than she did in her previous job.

Carol was devastated by the sudden death of her husband after thirty-five years of marriage. The pain and loneliness she suffered motivated her to begin a support group in her church for other widows. Now her group is active in ministering to shut-ins and those in nursing homes. In giving, she finds incredible joy.

Carly dreaded the thought of moving to a new city when her husband's firm relocated him. She had always lived close to her family and did not know anyone in the new town. To fill the time when her children were in school, she took some college courses and eventually went on to law school. Now she works for a Christian legal firm and finds deep fulfillment in combining her work with her ministry.

On a personal note, I was a jogger for fifteen years; I loved to run. I would run three to six miles and come home physically and mentally refreshed. It was a time, too, when I was able to pray and communicate with God. Then I injured my knee. I went to a doctor of sports medicine who drained the excess fluid from my swollen knee and suggested that I take a low-impact aerobics class to rehabilitate it. I was greatly disappointed, and I pleaded with God to allow me to run again. My knee, however, was just too fragile after the years of running.

To my surprise, I found I really enjoyed the aerobics classes. Eventually I became an aerobics instructor and six years ago began a free, community aerobics program at our church. The program has been very successful and I enjoy those classes even more than I did jogging. Though initially I was very unhappy about the change, once I accepted it God gave me a new and better direction.

If we accept the life changes that come, God is then able

to show us new doors of challenge. If we resist all change, we become stuck in the past, never able to move on to other things, always talking about the "good old days," unable to see the "good new future."

Besides accepting the changes that come into our life, we should *look* for new challenges that will stimulate us to grow. Because I had been such a controlling person, I decided I would really have to fight against this habit by forcing myself to do things I was afraid of doing. When we took our kids to amusement parks, I usually settled for the tamer rides, sitting on a bench while they went on all the "wild" rides with their dad. After my decision to embrace change, the kids asked if we could go to Ohio to two very large amusement parks for our vacation. I went on every roller coaster in those parks— even the ones that went in a 360-degree circle upside-down, and were called "death-defying." (It felt good to "defy death"!—Please understand, I'm not recommending wild rides for everyone, but it did work for me.)

I was also traveling quite a bit at that time, speaking for Christian women's groups and making TV appearances. I had always been an uptight traveler, wanting to know all the details in advance. Instead of making all the decisions concerning my accommodations, I decided to let my host church make those decisions for me. I was never sure who was going to meet me at the airport, or where I would be staying. This allowed me opportunity to look to God to care for me rather than trust in my own control. I found that I really began to enjoy travel and was not nearly as rigid and inflexible.

I went on to become a certified aerobics instructor at the age of forty-seven—a certification test that meant performing exercises in front of women who were in their twenties and had "great bodies." I also began Bible school at the age of fifty-one and am starting a new Bible study in a federal prison. I am really beginning to *enjoy* change and find it provides the "adrenalin" to both body and spirit that keeps me growing.

I believe the more secure a woman is, the more competent she feels and the less likely she will strive to be in control. Change helps to accomplish this goal. When a woman responds correctly to change, when she goes against her fears, and desire to control, she feels good about herself, which improves her self-image. She learns to trust in the grace of God, which is sufficient to meet every need. The freer she is to embrace change, the better she feels.

As women grow older, their human nature desires *more* security, not less. And if we don't learn to embrace change, we eventually will become frozen into fixed patterns of behavior. We all know older people who are imprisoned by habit patterns and whose lives and outlook grow narrower year after year.

In addition to accepting change in our life, we also need to learn the freedom of relinquishment.

## The Power of Relinquishment

Five years ago, I began to lose weight. My hair started thinning out and my eyes began to feel as if they were filled with sand. After my third visit to the ophthalmologist, he sent me to an endocrinologist who diagnosed Graves disease. It is a form of hyper-thyroidism and has become better known since Barbara Bush was diagnosed with it.

After the endocrinologist got my thyroid under control, I still suffered from eye problems and they began to enlarge and bulge. My doctor informed me that the eye disease was a related but separate problem that was difficult to treat, but hopefully would run its course. At that time I met two women who also had Graves disease and whose eyes unfortunately did not get better. In fact, their eyes became so enlarged that they had to have radical surgery to correct the problem.

I was worried. I didn't like the way my bulging eyes looked and I was concerned they would get worse. I cried, and prayed, and tried to turn over my condition to God—but I always came back to *worry*. I knew I had to completely trust God in this because I was in a situation over which neither I nor the doctors had any control. I could *only* look to God.

One Monday night I went to my weekly Bible study at the Drug Rehabilitation Center, and a new girl came walking up to me.

"Hi! Do you remember me?" she said brightly.

She looked familiar, but I couldn't remember her name. She told me that she had been to the center two years ago and her name was Donna.

"The last time I was in here you told me to go to the doctor because you thought I might have a thyroid problem, remember?" It was then that I really looked at her and realized her eyes were quite large and bulging.

"Yes, I remember," I replied. "Did you go?"

"Yes, and I want to thank you, because I'm under treatment now for Graves disease. I never would have gone if you hadn't mentioned it."

As she talked, I was mesmerized by her eyes. They were *very* large, exactly the way I was afraid mine would get. But a funny thing happened. It was like looking right at my *fear*—and it didn't seem so frightening. As Donna continued to tell me about her treatment, I was sending up a silent prayer of relinquishment to God. *God, if you allow my eyes to look like that, it's okay. I want to release my fear and accept your will in this area of my life.*

I forgot about my prayer—until about a month later when I realized that my eyes were completely normal again. As I thought back, I was sure my eyes had begun to get better that night when I released my fear to God. I'd hardly even *thought* about my eyes for a month!

I believe that our control over a situation through fear and worry keeps God *out*. When we give our fears to Him and trust Him like a baby trusts his mother, it activates His power to bring about the best possible answer. In this case it was healing. But I was also willing to accept whatever God had for me. After all my difficulties with control, I'd slowly learned that His will is for my greatest good, no matter what it is.

In fact, it's generally true that the more power we have in a situation, the less power God has—and the less power we have, the more power God has. So then, when we are powerless, we can know that God is in control. Paul said it best: "For when I am weak, then I am strong—the less I have, the more I depend on him" (2 Corinthians 12:10b, TLB).

I experienced the truth of that statement when our son Tom left home after a confrontation about his drug problem. (This is covered more fully in my book, *No Two Alike*.) My husband told Tom he had to either abide by our rules or leave. He left.

I went to church that night and prayed, "God, I have no control over Tom's life. I don't even know where he is, but you are in total control."

Gradually, I felt the burden of responsibility for Tom lift off my shoulders, and I was able to praise God with real freedom. I was still concerned about his safety, but the *panic* had left my soul.

We didn't hear from Tom for several days but, amazingly, I slept soundly every night. I knew that the God of the universe could look after Tom—certainly better than I could under the circumstances! After three days, Tom called his father and asked if he could come home. That was the turning point.

Today, Tom is a strong Christian serving God as leader of our large kids'-church ministry. Sometimes I wonder what would have happened if I had continued to assume the burden of responsibility for Tom's life—chasing him, hounding him to come home, bombarding him with scripture verses—instead of leaving him in God's hands. I wonder how many of us limit God in situations through our worry and control.

Jennifer found out the hard way how we can block God's work. She and Sam had been married for ten years when they became Christians. Jennifer was sure that now their marriage would be different, because Sam had been a drug addict for most of their married life. Instead, Sam now went to church *high*. Their life was filled with the same quarrels and arguments about Sam's addiction—Sam would threaten to leave, Jennifer would beg him to stay, Sam would promise to stop taking drugs, and for a few months there would be peace. Then Sam would get high again. The pastor of their church prayed for him to be delivered from his addiction, but to no avail.

Finally, Sam left Jennifer and moved in with another woman. One week later, Jennifer found out she was pregnant. For the first time in her life Jennifer had no one else's problems to occupy her mind. Growing up she'd been mostly occupied with her father's alcoholism. Then, in her marriage, all her focus had been on Sam's addiction. Now she saw that she was the one in need of help.

Jennifer and Sam were separated six months, and during that time she learned to release him to God by letting go of her fears and anger. That required looking away from Sam and looking up to the Lord. She finally felt free from a sense of responsibility for his addiction.

Sam moved back home just before the birth of the baby, but continued his pattern of getting high on drugs. Jennifer, however, was no longer affected by it and did not feel the responsibility to make him get better. She was resting in the fact that God was in charge.

One night after Jennifer had gone to bed, Sam sat up and watched a late movie about a drug-addict. As Sam watched how addiction destroyed the man's family, he was overcome with the destructiveness of his own habit. The power of the Holy Spirit brought Sam to his knees, and he sobbed out his sin before God and asked forgiveness. When Sam stood up again, he was a changed man. All this took place twenty feet away from Jennifer's bedroom—where she slept soundly, unaware that God accomplished in five minutes what she had attempted to do during fifteen years of marriage.

A few months after his deliverance Sam and Jennifer joined our church. He has remained drug-free, and more important, he has become a truly committed Christian.

Ginger also learned the power of relinquishment—but it took her eight years. She joined our fellowship soon after she graduated from high school, and before long fell in love with Dave, one of the single men in the church. They dated infrequently over the next seven years, and though Ginger was in love with him, Dave was not committed to her.

Finally Ginger gave up on Dave, and began dating another young man. Soon they were engaged and set the date for a summer wedding. Six weeks before the wedding, Ginger faced the fact that she was still in love with Dave and just couldn't marry this man on the rebound. So in spite of the tremendous embarrassment she called off the wedding.

Ginger decided to go for counseling with one of the women in our church, who advised her to go to Dave and admit that she was still in love with him, but then to ask him for a release—an odd sort of directive. The next evening, Ginger stopped by Dave's house after work and told him of her feelings. He told her that he did care about her, but didn't feel he could make a lifetime commitment to her.

Ginger went back home and spent some time on her knees. She lifted her hands to God as if symbolically handing Dave over to God. At that moment, she knew she had truly released Dave and her feelings to God—and with him, her dreams of love and marriage.

Three days later, she was at work when she got a phone call from Dave. He told her that he really did love her and wanted to get back together. She was so shocked that she burst into tears. The other women in the office thought she must have received tragic news.

Today, Ginger and Dave have been married for more than three years. Recently when we were discussing her story, I asked her why it had taken eight years to give her feelings about Dave to the Lord. She replied, "My attitude toward God had always been that He owed me something, because I had a very unhappy childhood in a series of foster homes. I always thought God *owed* me because He allowed me to have such a rotten childhood. In fact, I had a hard time giving up the idea of anything I thought I should have. But hopefully I'm learning that God does want the best for me—even if life is not always the way I think it should be at the moment."

In all three of these stories about releasing feelings, people, and problems to God, there is a similar pattern: We are confronted with a problem; we struggle with acceptance for months or years; we finally release it and accept God's will. Then He acts. Remember, however, that *releasing* is not another way to force God's hand to get what we want. It is final and complete acceptance of God's will, whatever it is, and whether circumstances come around to our way or not.

When I was a very new Christian, I made the acquaintance of a young woman who had been a missionary for a number of years in South America. She and her husband and three-year-old son had come home because she was diagnosed with cancer. I had the privilege of spending a lot of time with her the last year of her life. She came from a godly family and we all—her family, friends, and pastor—believed that she was going to be healed. When she died, I was devastated. I couldn't believe God would let this very committed thirty-year-old woman die. I wondered how her pastor would handle the funeral and really didn't want to attend.

Her pastor, who had fervently believed in her healing, preached from Hebrews 12:39–40:

> And these men of faith, though they trusted God and won his approval, none of them received *all* that God had promised them; for God wanted them to wait and share the even better rewards that were prepared for us. (TLB, italics added)

We won't always get the answer *we* want, because God foresees something better for us. And when we give up our control we are saying, "God, I accept your will for me because I know that you desire the best for me and I trust in your unchanging nature" (see James 1:17). We affirm the truth of Scripture:

> For I know the plans I have for you, declares the Lord, plans to prosper you and not to harm you, plans to give you hope and a future (Jeremiah 29:11).

In fact, learning to trust in the goodness of God is the opposite of control.

## Who *Really* Is in Control?

Judith Rodin, psychologist at Yale University, has been involved in much of the recent research on control. She says that "feelings of control and self-determination are 'of central importance in influencing psychological and physical health and perhaps even longevity in older adults.' "[4] Those people who feel they have no control over what happens to them develop a pessimistic attitude toward life, and the stress engendered may actually suppress the immune system and shorten their life.

We women are often exhorted to "take control of our lives" as the answer to most of the problems we face. We are assured that once *we* are in control, we will be happier, healthier and certainly no one will ever take advantage of us.

Unfortunately, each one of us will face circumstances over which we have *no* control—death, accidents, the choices of another person, broken relationships, physical illness, war, natural catastrophes, even higher gas prices. All of these things may take us by surprise, a shattering reminder of how little control we really have.

*To think that we have control is an illusion.* Ultimately, our God is sovereign. Even though God, through Jesus, has given us Christians a measure of His authority (Matthew 28:19–20), it is only to reinforce *His* will on this earth, never our own will. Scripture tells us that "in his heart a man plans his course, but the Lord determines his steps" (Proverbs 16:9), and that "the Lord works out everything for his *own* ends—even the wicked for a day of disaster" (Proverbs 16:4, italics added).

This generation of Christians is discovering that God has

---

[4]Robert J. Trotter, "Regaining Control," *Longevity* (Dec. 89/Jan.90), pp. 60–62, 66.

called us to be co-workers with Him in bringing His kingdom to reign on the earth. We are learning how to tear down strongholds with prayer (2 Corinthians 10:4), and to bind demonic forces by praise (Psalm 149:6–9). But in discovering our rights as children of the King, we too often step over the line and actually try to control God.

In the life of Jesus are two small incidents that speak volumes about the desire to control. The first is in John chapter 2, and took place at the wedding feast at Cana. In reply to His mother's request to "do" something, Jesus said, "Dear woman, why do you involve me? My time has not yet come."

The second incident, also in John, was when Jesus' brothers told Him to go to Judea to the Feast of Tabernacles to display His miraculous power. Jesus replied, "You go to the Feast, I am not yet going up to this Feast, because for me the right time has not yet come" (John 7:8).

In both instances Jesus said *no* to the request—but afterward He *did* change the water into wine, and after His brothers left, He *did* go the Feast in Judea. Was Jesus doubleminded? How could the One who said, "Let your 'Yes' be 'Yes,' and your 'No,' 'No,'" violate His own word?

I believe that Jesus said no originally because His actions were not determined by human need or another's request—His actions and their timing were solely determined by the will of the Father. His response was no to his mother and brothers, but His Father communicated to Him His will to change the water into wine and to go the Feast.

The Creator will not be dictated to by His creatures (Isaiah 45:11), but we have been allowed to be co-workers with Him in carrying out *His* will. There will be things that we don't understand in this life, but the Scriptures encourage us: "Since the Lord is directing our steps, why try to understand everything that happens along the way?" (Proverbs 20:24, TLB). The prophet Habakkuk had to learn this lesson in his lifetime also.

Habakkuk lived at the end of a generation that had enjoyed peace and prosperity because of God's favor toward the godly King Josiah (2 Kings 22:12–17). However, that society had deteriorated into one where greed was the motivating force and the poor were exploited. Now they faced imminent change in their political, economic and religious lives. In fact, the name Habakkuk comes from the Hebrew word *habhak*, to embrace, and he certainly had to learn to embrace the change that came in his lifetime.

We can easily put ourselves in Habakkuk's place. In America, we are in the midst of prosperity that has come to us because of God's favor and blessing. But we too stand at a frightening crossroad of change.

Habakkuk began to cry out to God and even accuse God of not listening to him. Basically, his first question was, "Why do the wicked prosper, while the righteous are exploited?" It was the same question that prompted Rabbi Harold Kushner to write his best-selling book, *When Bad Things Happen to Good People.* The thing that really bothered Habakkuk was that God seemed indifferent to what was happening, and even though he had prayed long and hard (Habakkuk 1:2), God did not seem to listen. Finally God answered Habakkuk: He was not indifferent, but had been working behind the scenes to raise up the Babylonians as His means of judging His people for their sins (1:6).

Now Habakkuk *really* had a problem! How could a holy God use evil people to judge Israel? Habakkuk decided he would suspend his limited perceptions and wait for God to answer him (2:1). There is probably nothing harder for us than to wait on God. Waiting means an end to all our human activity and control. It means that we are helpless to do anything, and that God really is in control of this universe—and our lives.

God never directly answered Habakkuk's question, but He did tell him that the Babylonians would eventually be punished and overthrown. This section of Scripture (2:2–20) contains one of the mightiest verses on faith in the Bible—a verse that prompted Martin Luther to reexamine his own theology, with momentous consequences for the Reformation. The verse is quoted three times in the New Testament: "But the righteous will live by his faith" (2:4b).

"Faith is the key to unanswered prayer," writes Bible scholar Cyril Barber. "It is grounded in the conviction that God hears and answers prayer and eventually will reward those who diligently seek Him . . . Faith is the key to a correct view of history, for through faith the believer recognizes that God will work all things out according to the counsel of His perfect will."[5]

---

[5]Cyril J. Barber, *Habakkuk and Zephaniah* (Chicago, Ill.: Moody Press, 1985), pp. 46, 47.

God's reply to Habakkuk ends with the statement: "But the Lord is in his holy temple. . . ." (2:20). In other words, God still rules this universe. No matter how it looks, God is on the throne. In this age of humanism, when we have elevated man as god, we need to remember that God is sovereign, He is still in control.

That realization immediately led Habakkuk into a beautiful psalm, which is said to be "*on shigionoth*, a rare term (Psalm 7:1) used only in cases of complete reliance on God's faithfulness."[6] After recounting God's glorious faithfulness in Israel's past history, Habakkuk realized that there was *nothing he could do but wait*—in spite of his *fear* of the coming invasion, in spite of his *anger* at the injustices around him, in spite of his *shame* for the sins of his nation—he made a decision to "wait patiently for the day of calamity" (3:16b). This was no passive kind of resignation—"whatever will be will be"—this was an active dependence on God, demonstrated by his praise.

The short book of Habakkuk ends with the greatest declaration of faith in the Bible (3:17–19). Even though all the things that Judah depended on for her survival should fail, Habakkuk could rejoice in God. His rejoicing springs from his relationship with God, a covenant God who keeps His promises and who will provide the stamina to not only endure hardship but to walk on the "heights" (v. 19). Habakkuk saw that God truly is in control.

Some years ago, when I first discovered this wonderful book of the Bible, I saw in the three short chapters an action plan to release control no matter what the situation.

First, we need to confess our fear, anger and doubts to God. After all, He knows what is in our heart. Those negative emotions can only hurt us when we refuse to recognize them. But once we pour our heart out to the Lord, He can heal us. God did not chastise Habakkuk for his anger, and He will not chastise us. Our confession will open the way to fellowship with God.

Secondly, Habakkuk waited on God. We also need to learn to wait until we hear from God. Perhaps God will give us a Bible verse, speak to us through a friend, a book, a sermon or even a song. Sometimes we may wait years for an answer to

---

[6]David W. Baker, *Nahum, Habakkuk, Zephaniah* (Downers Grove, Ill.: Inter-Varsity Press, 1988), p. 68.

our prayer, but while we wait God will continually encourage us to trust.

On the way to the grocery store the other day, I was praying about a long-term situation, only half-listening to the Christian songs on my car radio. Almost immediately after I had prayed about my concern for the three-hundredth time, contemporary artist Twila Paris began singing about trusting God. The words of the song immediately lifted me from my worry, and reminded me to refocus on God.

Thirdly, make a decision to trust God in spite of circumstances. Habakkuk never received the answer he was asking of God, but his vision was lifted from the problem to the majesty of God in His temple. Habakkuk said that in spite of the circumstances: "I *will* rejoice in the Lord, I *will* be joyful in God my Savior" (3:18). We need to make the same decision.

When I am attempting to release my control over a situation and surrender it to God, it seems I get bombarded with negative thoughts. When my daughter, Shannon, moved into the city of Chicago, I suddenly became aware of all the crime statistics. In one weekend alone, there were sixty-five shootings—to say nothing of the rapes, burglaries and muggings. When I heard or read about these crimes, I would immediately think about her living all alone in that violent city, and it was easy for me to fall into worry and fear.

But I made a decision to trust God for her safety. That meant when I heard anything negative (which would usually send me on my pessimistic mode of thinking), I would say quietly in my thoughts: *Father, I give Shannon over to your protection and reject worry and fear. I praise you for your care over her life.* I had to say that *a lot* in the beginning, but little by little I received God's peace. Shannon has lived in the city for five years and God *has* protected her. I must admit that once a man attempted to grab her from behind in the hallway of her building—but she was quick-witted enough to elbow him in the ribs and scream at the top of her lungs. He quickly exited the building. And I give thanks to God for His continued protection.

At the beginning of this section I referred to the recent research about control indicating that people who feel they have *no control* over what happens to them will suffer negative consequences. You may ask, "How do we escape those negative consequences when we give up control?" As Christians, we are not releasing control to "fate," hoping for the best. Rather, we are turning over our shortsighted attempt to control our destiny and that of others to the sovereign God, who really does rule this universe, and is interested in our lives. Our attempt to control is motivated by fear, anger, shame, and doubt, but our release of that control brings true security because our life is in God's hands.

I used to have a poster over my desk of a little child leaning into a very large hand cupped around his body. The look on the child's face was one of pure peace, supreme trust. When I glanced at the poster, I reminded myself that that was what God wanted me to do—release all my manipulations and schemes and rest completely in Him. The popular folk-song says, "He's got the whole world in His hands."

And He really does.

A national woman's magazine recently published the results of a survey among 3000 women in an article entitled: *Men Trouble*. The results showed that women's opinion of men has reached "an all-time low."[7] After twenty-five years of the women's revolution, we are further apart than ever. The cover of the magazine said: "Men are still rats." This is the attitude that has caused women to reach out and take control, and by the looks of things, be more firmly entrenched in that control than ever.

Malachi is the last book in the Old Testament, and the last statement in that book is about the return of the prophet Elijah who "will turn the hearts of the fathers to their children, and the hearts of the children to their fathers. . . ." (Malachi 4:6). Many believe we are entering a time when we will literally see the fulfillment of this scripture. The nuclear family has dissolved like the elements in an atomic blast. Children are the fallout from divorce, separation, and the battle of the sexes. And women have risen from those ashes to take control, to prove that they "can get along fine without a man, thank you."

Into this ravaged landscape strides the "spirit of Elijah" to restore what has been lost, to turn the father's heart toward his children, to take up his lost position of priest and head in the home. But we women have to "let go." The man can't move into his position if we stand in the way.

---

[7]Nina Keilin, "Men Trouble," *Ladies' Home Journal* (August 1990), pp. 84–89.

And as Christian women, we have an awesome responsibility—we are going to have to turn away from the world's propaganda, the feminist shibboleths, from anxiety and fear in a hostile world, and once again learn to trust. To trust our husband, to trust the authority structure in the Word of God, and most of all to trust in our heavenly Father who really does "work for the good of those who love him" (Romans 8:28).

I'm ready for the change! How about you?